New Techniques for
5 STRING BANJO

Volume 1 – Beginner

JEFF BELDING

Editing by: Ronny Schiff

Design by Charylu Roberts and O.Ruby Productions

Cover Design by: www.fiverr.com/josepepitojr

Illustrations and Figures by: www.fiverr.com/medgrafix

GUITAR
BANJO
MANDOLIN
FIDDLE
MUSIC
ALONG THE WAY

ISBN 978-0-578-42991-5

More information about the audio access that accompanies this book is
available at www.jeffbelding.com

Dedication

To my dear wife Edwina and my daughters, Joanna and Valerie...

You have all been so supportive of my music, and my unconventional way of making a living in a business that has so many ups and downs. But through all those years, you never complained. You all just gave me more of your love!

To my parents Bob and Edith Belding...

*Thanks for never pressuring me into getting a "real" job!
Thanks to my Dad for sharing great music with me.
Someday we will play together again...Rest in Peace Dad.*

And to my sweet sister Dianna...

*Without you in my life, I may never have taken notice of all that great music on your stereo—the Beatles, Roy Orbison, Petula Clark, The Searchers, and the list goes on and on!
Thanks for giving a nerdy kid like me some confidence and sense of self-worth.
I lost you far too soon, but your kind and loving spirit will be with me always.*

Acknowledgments

The following are those I consider responsible for inspiring and encouraging me to write this book: Edwina Belding, Roger Sprung, Bill Keith, Earl Scruggs, Jack Dugan, Chris Dunn, Lorain Hilton-Van Zandt, Sue Brooke, Keith Medlin, Jack Fragomeni, Robert Belding, Lou Mulligan, MuseScore, Dominic Francese, Sr., Ken Evans and all of my great friends at the NWA. Also, members of the following groups have each had a significant role in making me a better banjo player: Stockade, Orion, Out of the Bluegrass, Synergy, The Bronco Boys, Saratoga Faire, The Spirites Consort, The Moonshiners, and Craig Thaler. Thanks to all of my students throughout the years! Teaching you has been the ultimate learning experience for me.

Table of Contents

Banjo Figures

Introduction

Hallelujah! I just took a banjo lesson from myself for the first time. That may sound a little weird to some of you, but how else would I know that this book *really* works!
It may sound like I'm bragging, but after 40 years of teaching the banjo and other string instruments, I'd like to think that I know what the heck I'm doing by now.

This book is the culmination of what has worked for my students as well as what has *not*. Let's face it, most people who take up a musical instrument are doing it for the fun of it and as a hobby. However, that doesn't mean that they don't deserve the same thrill of playing music as the big star on the stage of the Grand Ole Opry.

I think we all know that everyone has their own learning curve when it comes to any activity that they take on. I've had the fullest range of students that one could imagine. There are the super talented ones who pick up everything as fast as I can explain it. There are those who can barely make a sound by pressing down on a string and take weeks to just make *that* happen. And then there are those who are about average, and, with practice and dedication, in time they show amazing results in their abilities.

I would like to think that I have designed this book for all three of the aforementioned categories. Like I have said, after years of teaching banjo, I have learned to move slowly enough for anyone to hopefully "get it."

You might well ask: "Why the title? What are these new techniques for banjo of which you speak?" Okay, maybe my banjo licks are not necessarily something new or totally original, but I would like to think that I have a new approach that will get you playing sooner and more efficiently.

I chose tablature as my main vehicle of notation in this book. In all of the other string instruments that I teach, I do stress the use of music notation. However, outside of classical five-string banjo players, tablature has taken over as the standard language.

That is not to say that this is an "anti-music" book in which you learn tunes by rote memory and then try to parrot them as best you can. Wherever possible, I tried to give musical explanations when they are called for. The primary "Music Theory" aspect of this book is about rhythm and good solid timing. This is something that every banjo player needs in order to survive in the world of music and of course jamming. More involved Music Theory appears in future volumes of this series.

So, put on your banjo picks (*the right way!*), and I hope you enjoy this ride as much as I have in the construction of it.

Thanks to all of my students! Past, present, and future!

CHAPTER 1

SET-UP AND PREPARATION

Parts of the Banjo (Lower)

This figure shows you some of the most important parts of the banjo, mostly in the lower (circular) area. However, growing up from that circle is what is known as the "Neck."

So, if you are to put human attributes to your banjo, the circular section is the "torso," the long straight section is the "neck," and it even has a "head" at the top of the neck (not to confuse the actual "head," with the "drumhead" that takes up just about the entire circular section).

The "resonator" is found on the back of most "bluegrass banjos." Its purpose is for greater sound projection, but some still prefer the "open-back" banjo for its looks and to cut down on added weight.

The "tension lugs" are evenly spaced around the circle and they are for tightening the drumhead, using a standard "drum key." For now, that's probably a job for your local music store technician.

The "bridge" has a lot to do with locating the placement of the picking hand. It is movable, but again, leave that up to the professionals as to its correct location.

The "tailpiece" is where the strings are attached first and then they pass over the bridge, up the neck and into the tuning pegs at the top of the banjo. You may ask, "What about changing strings?" Best to have your local music store do them. *(I do change my own strings, but I derive no pleasure from the activity.)*

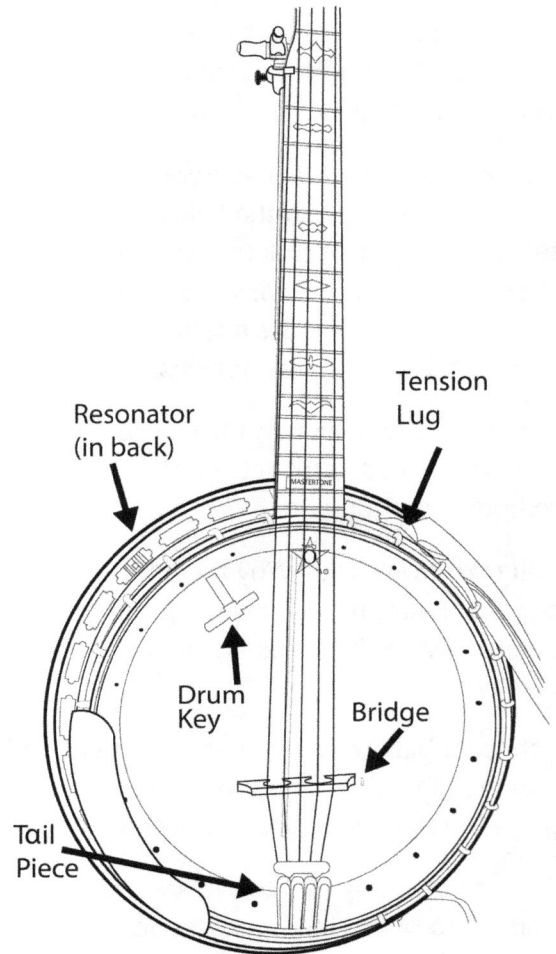

Figure 1. Parts of the Banjo Lower Section

About Tuning

Tuning can be a mysterious and challenging process for the beginning banjoist. Being in tune is, of course, very important. For starters, do the following:

When you buy your first banjo, before you leave the store, have it tuned by someone who knows how to do it. At least that way, it's in the ballpark by the time you get it home.

Speaking of buying your first banjo, ask the salesperson if they include an electronic tuner in the purchase. It's a crafty way to maybe get them to throw one in with the deal. If they don't, it's highly recommended that you buy one anyway.

Electronic tuners are useful tools, but they do not possess magical powers. They only serve a purpose when you know how to use them properly. Once you learn how to use one, getting your banjo in tune should always be done before beginning to play.

If you have never played an instrument before, then having it "professionally" tuned at your local music store is your best course of action for getting started with this book. Specifically ask for "G tuning." As you learn more basics about the operation of your banjo and, as your "musical ear" develops, you will find that there are non-electronic methods of tuning that will help you as well.

Appendix B provides additional insights into tuning.

About the Banjo Strap

Here is what you need to know about the best placement and most efficient use of the banjo strap.

Your basic banjo strap looks much like a guitar strap, except that it has a hook at each end like a small D clamp. Some straps have ties at each end, but the function is the same.

The tricky part is where to place those hooks to get the best balance. Many banjos come with a built-in "eyelet," which is where you are "supposed" to place the hooks. You will find one near the tailpiece and one near the bottom of the neck.

Go ahead and hook up to the tension lug or the eyelet near the tailpiece, but don't even bother hooking up to the one next to the neck. The banjo won't balance properly, and you'll end up having to hold the neck up while trying to play.

Instead bring that hook around the back of the banjo neck and hook it to the second or third tension lug. *This* will give you the balance that you need.

Another misstep that can occur with the strap is actually putting it over your head and letting it rest there with the banjo hanging from your neck. There is a second step to the process. You must bring your picking hand through the strap, thus letting the strap hang over *just* the shoulder of your fretting hand.

When seated, the strap should be adjusted short enough so the weight of the banjo is not on your legs, but suspended just high enough to be held up by the fretting hand shoulder. When standing, you must decide how far up or down you would like the banjo to go. By some miracle, my strap ended up being adjusted just one length that works for me sitting or standing.

One final piece of advice: please don't buy the "bargain basement" strap. Most banjos are quite heavy, and you need a nice strong piece of leather to stand up to the weight.

This illustration shows how the strap should be attached to the banjo.

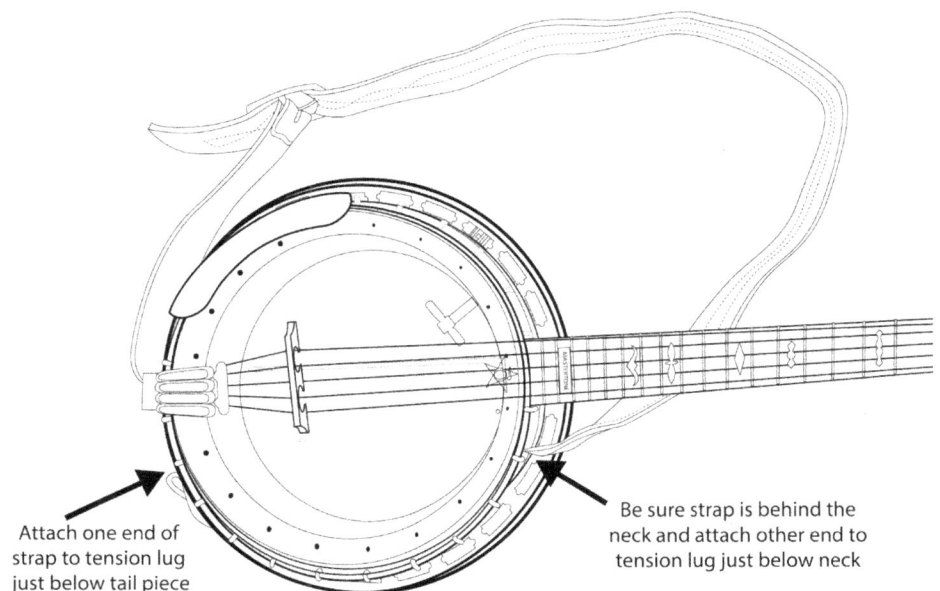

Attach one end of strap to tension lug just below tail piece

Be sure strap is behind the neck and attach other end to tension lug just below neck

Figure 2. The Banjo Strap

About Fingerpicks

A banjo is "picked" using three "fingerpicks" attached to three fingers of the "picking hand."

If you are right-handed, the fingerpicks go on the right hand, and if you are left-handed (with a banjo set up specifically for left-handers), they go on your left hand. To avoid confusion between "north- and south-paws," this hand is referred to as the "picking hand" from here on.

Your set of three banjo picks includes two identical metal picks for your index and middle fingers, and one thumb pick for your (you guessed it!) thumb.

Most thumb picks are made entirely of plastic, and come in three possible sizes of small, medium, and large. Try the various sizes out at your local music store. *(I use a brass "Acri" (brand name) thumb pick with a plastic appendage for the actual picking part of it.)*

The two metal finger picks are made of pliable metal, so they can be "shaped" around your index and middle fingers. These two fingers are a little different in size and shape, so it's a good idea to mark one of the picks with a permanent marker and leave one plain so you can dependably know which one best fits which finger. *(Again, I use Acri fingerpicks as well. I find them very comfortable over the more basic store-bought pick.)* If you do buy more "generic" fingerpicks, try to find a thickness of .025. Some banjos come with a set of three picks, but they may be too poorly made to be worth your while. The Acri picks (you can Google Acri banjo picks) are a bit pricey, but well worth it.

And now, take a look at the pictures on the next page. Many times a new student has started out putting their picks on the wrong way, so there are right and wrong photos for fingerpick and thumb pick placement.

When putting on fingerpicks be sure the "pick" part is on the fleshy side of the finger, not on the fingernail side. Adjust the back of the fingerpick around your finger tip to ensure a good grip.

The thumb pick should just form-fit naturally around your thumb. If it does not feel like a nice smooth fit, it must be backward.

Okay, you've had your banjo tuned, you have your fingerpicks on correctly, and you have your banjo strap secured. For now, use your thumb pick, picking in a downward motion (towards the floor) to pick any given string. Let us continue…

Fingerpick Placement

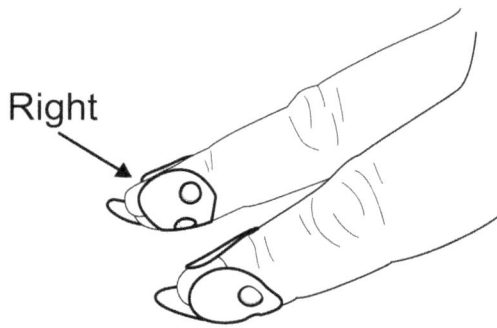

Right

Figure 3. Fingerpicks—Right

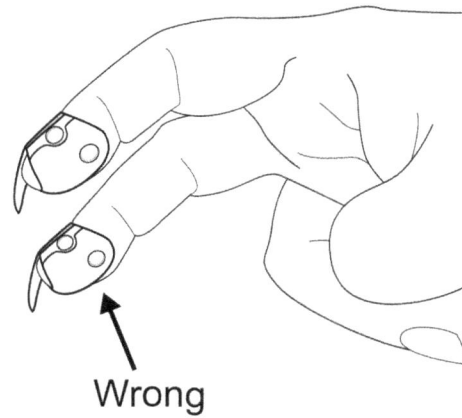

Wrong

Figure 4. Fingerpicks—Wrong

Thumb Pick Placement

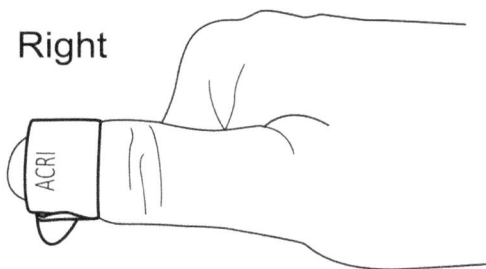

Right

ACRI

Figure 5. Thumb Pick—Right

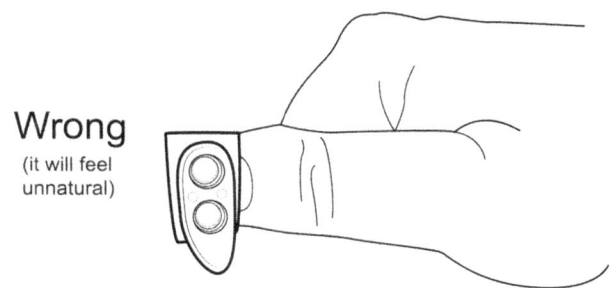

Wrong
(it will feel unnatural)

Figure 6. Thumb Pick—Wrong

READING TABLATURE AND COUNTING TIME

How to Read Banjo Tablature

PART 1

- The banjo tablature staff consists of five lines, which represent the five strings of the banjo.

- A zero on the staff indicates an open string. A string is said to be "open," when no fingers are pushing down on that string.

- The tablature (TAB) staff below shows each of the open string's letter names and numbers.

- The illustration shows the location of these strings on the banjo neck.

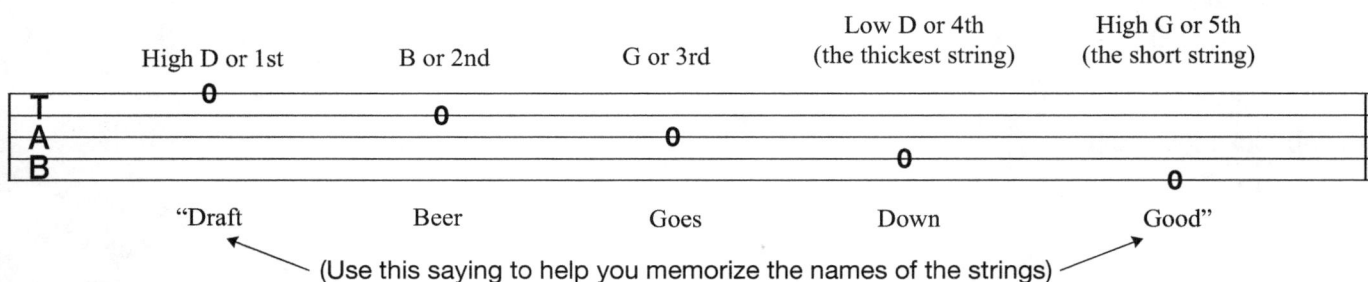

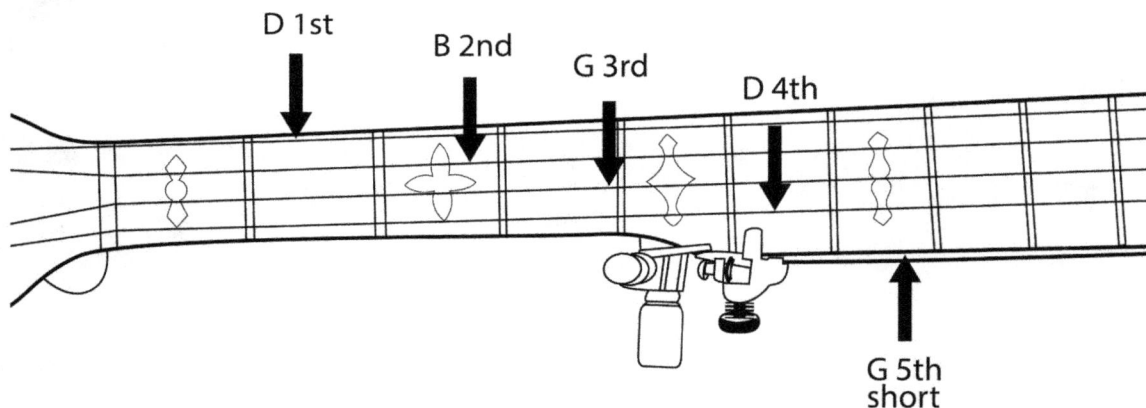

| High D or 1st | B or 2nd | G or 3rd | Low D or 4th (the thickest string) | High G or 5th (the short string) |

```
T  ──0────────────────────────────────────────────────────────────
A  ─────────────0──────────────────────────────────────────────────
B  ─────────────────────0───────────────0──────────────────────────
   ───────────────────────────────────────────────────0────────────
```

| "Draft | Beer | Goes | Down | Good" |

(Use this saying to help you memorize the names of the strings)

Figure 7. Names and Numbers of the Open Strings on the Banjo Neck

- For now, your banjo music is broken down into "measures" of eight even beats. Each beat is a separate note of the measure.

- Each "note" is called an "eighth note" (one-eighth of the measure).

- Each 8th note is one "beat" of a measure of eight eighth notes.

- Bar lines separate each measure of eight eighth notes.

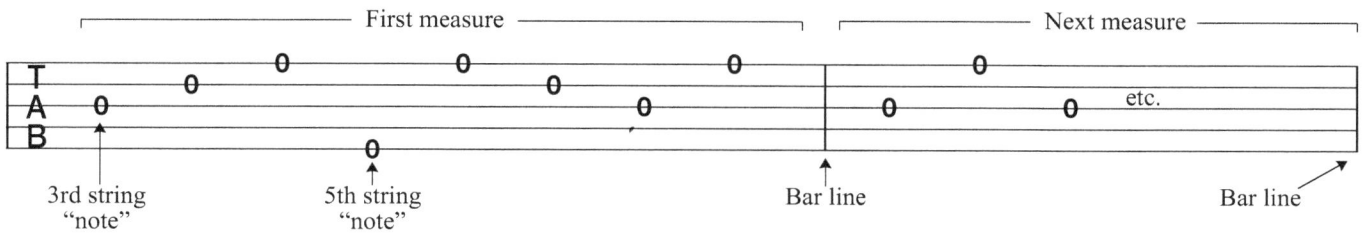

Figure 8. Parts of the Banjo Upper Section; Locating Frets

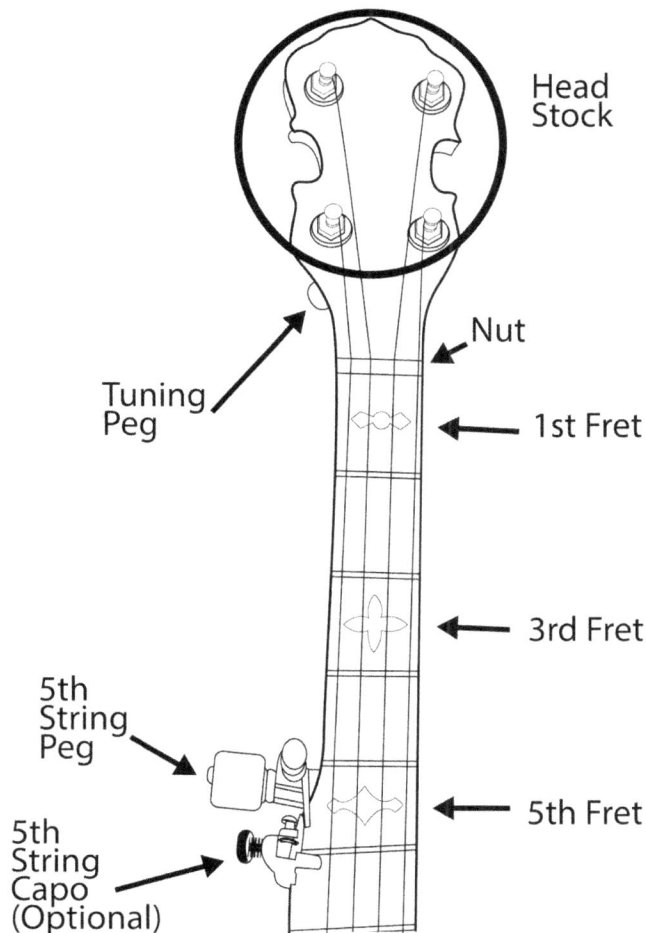

- The banjo neck is divided into sections called "frets"—see the diagram on the previous page.
  - Each "beat" is marked with a number that refers to the fret number to play on that beat.
  - Whatever line that fret number appears on tells you what string (str.) to pick—see the examples below:

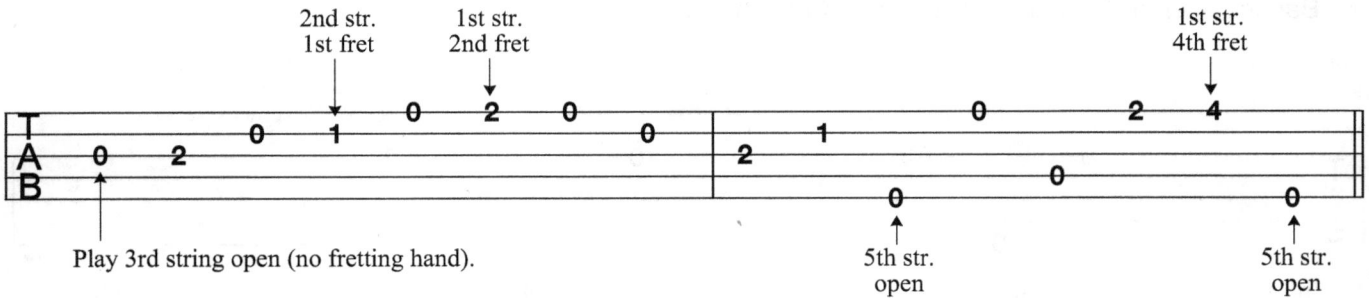

2nd str. 1st fret   1st str. 2nd fret   1st str. 4th fret

Play 3rd string open (no fretting hand).   5th str. open   5th str. open

PART 2

Tablature versus Standard Music Notation

The music staff and tab staff tell you two essential things: what note (or pitch) to play, and the rhythm of that note or series of notes (how fast or slow to play).

Eighth Notes and Quarter Notes

The following example shows how eighth notes and quarter notes appear in standard music notation (the top line) and tablature (the bottom line). It starts with eighth notes in the first measure, since most five-string banjo music *is* eighth-note driven. As you can see, there are 8 eighth notes in the first measure. Simply put, they are the faster notes. The second measure contains 4 quarter notes. They move exactly TWICE as slow as the eighth notes. On the audio, you will be able to hear the difference between the two.

"D" note   Eighth notes: (faster)   Quarter notes: (slower)   Eighth notes   Quarter notes

Here is the exact same series of notes in the language of *standard tablature notation:*

"D" note

A New Approach to Reading Tablature

This book uses a unique version of simplified tablature by eliminating the vertical and horizontal lines associated with standard tablature notation. In this new approach to tablature, when the notes come one after the other with no spaces in-between, they are the "faster" eighth notes. If the note is followed by an "X" on the center line of the staff, then the player must pause ("put on the brakes") to get the effect of the "slower" quarter notes.

The following example shows how this newly-simplified tablature compares to the music staff:

Eighth notes   Quarter notes

"Jeff's version"   (Put on the brakes!)

```
T 0 0 0 0 0 0 0 0 | 0   0   0   0 | 0 0 0 0 0 0 0 0 | 0   0   0   0
A                 |   x   x   x   |                 |     x   x   x   x
B                 |                |                 |
```

pause

From here on out, the music notation line will be eliminated, and "Jeff's" version of tab will be all that you see.

Half Notes

Relax...take your time, it's a *half note*. Half notes are held out twice as long as quarter notes. Two half notes can fit in a single measure of four beats.

The following is a comparison of eighth notes, quarter notes, and finally, half notes:

Here is the same in standard banjo tab notation:

```
T 0 0 0 0 0 0 0 0 | 0   0   0   0 | 0       0 | 0       0
A                 |                |           |
B                 |                |           |
```

Eighth notes: (quick)   Quarter notes: (slower)   Half notes: (slower yet!)

And finally, Jeff's version:

```
T 0 0 0 0 0 0 0 0 | 0   0   0   0 | 0       0 | 0       0
A                 |   x   x   x   x |  x R  x R |  x R  x R
B                 |                 |           |
```

"Relax"   "Relax"   "Relax"   "Relax"

And so, tablature in this book uses the upper case "R" in conjunction with the "x" to represent half notes. These then stretch the tempo out even further than the quarter notes.

Once again, the banjo tab line using "Jeff's version" is all you will see from here on in the book. If you are looking at other books in standard tablature notation, you have a key for interpreting them as well. Many authors have their own variations on tablature, and they will usually take the time to provide you with their own explanations.

PART 3

Skip to My Lou—Quarter Notes, Eighth Notes, and Half Notes

Don't worry about which fingers to pick with at this point. You can use just thumb if you like, or
any combination of thumb and fingers that feels right for now.

"Repeat sign":
Go to beginning
and repeat the tune.

About Repeat Signs

Start   Play through to these two dots

Go back to the opposite 2 dots,
and play entire section again.

First and second endings: Play through the 1st time (Repeat)   Skip to here 2nd time

1.   2.

(skip)   (keep going)

Leave out the 2nd time

The Repeat Measure Sign: Repeat everything   Repeat all those notes
                                   from previous measure   yet again

Final bar line
marks the end of a tune.
(Notice, NO dots…)

How to Count Time

Keeping good solid time is the key to becoming a good banjo player. Tapping your foot to each quarter note (note + X) is a good way to start.

Try the next Exercise (Exercise 1) tapping your foot evenly to each note you see. Then, repeat the exercise, counting the numbers (1 thru 4) written above.

M = (Pick with middle throughout)

Now, say the following out loud: "1 and 2 and 3 and 4 and." Tap your foot on "1, 2, 3, 4" while the word "and" is said during the pauses (Xs). Try saying the "out loud" exercises while tapping your foot on only the "1, 2, 3, 4." You may find this a little difficult, but it is a great skill to develop for keeping good time.

In Exercise 2, you will find the same series of notes, but the "and" beats have been added. When showing these counts in the Tab, the word "and" is replaced with the plus (+) sign, but you still say it as "and."

M throughout

Exercise 3 is all eighth notes. They will be played *twice* as fast as the notes in Exercise 2 (no pauses). Again, the foot should only tap on "1, 2, 3, 4" while the "+" (and) notes are between foot taps.

M throughout

CHAPTER 3

THE PICKING HAND

"Picking Hand" is used in order to avoid confusion for left-handed banjo players. Whether right or left, it's the hand that picks the strings. The thumb (TH) is assigned to pick the 5th, 4th, or 3rd Strings. It picks downward towards the floor.

The following exercise is for the thumb, picking various open strings. The abbreviations below the staff (TH), remind you to pick with your thumb.

The *Index Finger* (I), picks only the 2nd string for now. The *Middle Finger* (M), picks only the 1st string for now.

As you get into more advanced techniques, those rules will be subject to change.

The index and middle fingers both pick upwards toward your face. This is a good time to check if your picks are on correctly.

Here is an exercise for your index (I) and middle (M) fingers:

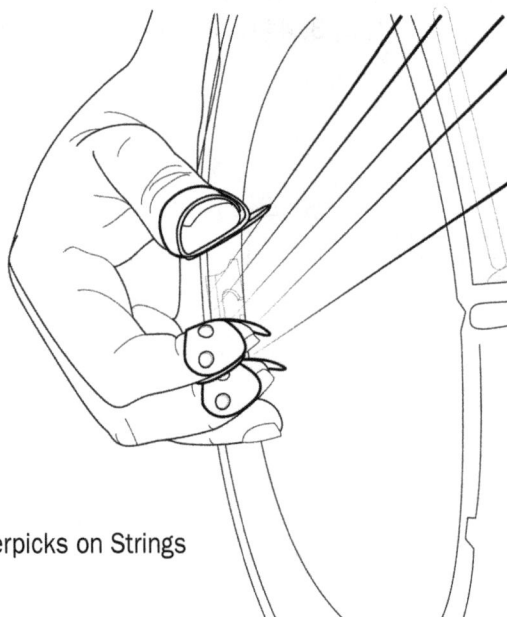

Figure 9. Fingerpicks on Strings

This is also a good time to check your picking hand position, and where to place your anchor fingers. The pinky and the ring finger should be touching the banjo head, near the bridge, as shown here:

Figure 10. Anchor Fingers Side View

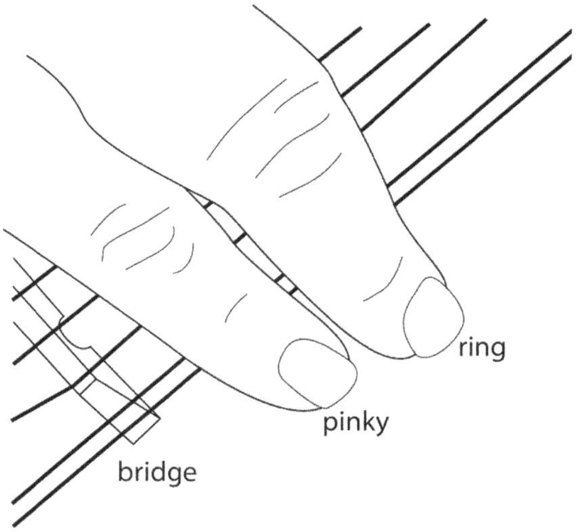

Figure 11. Anchor Fingers Close Up

Here is a picking exercise for all three fingers:

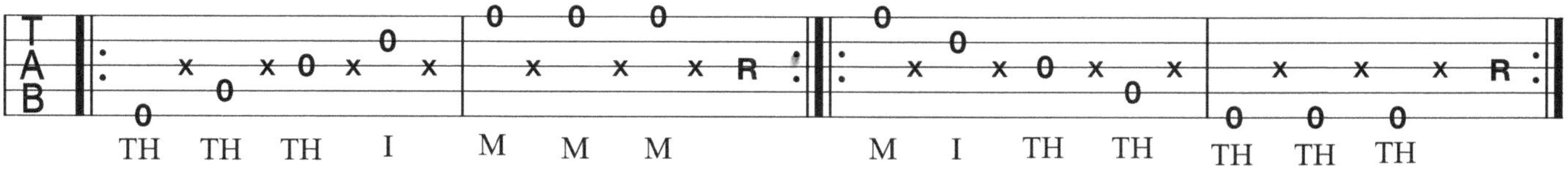

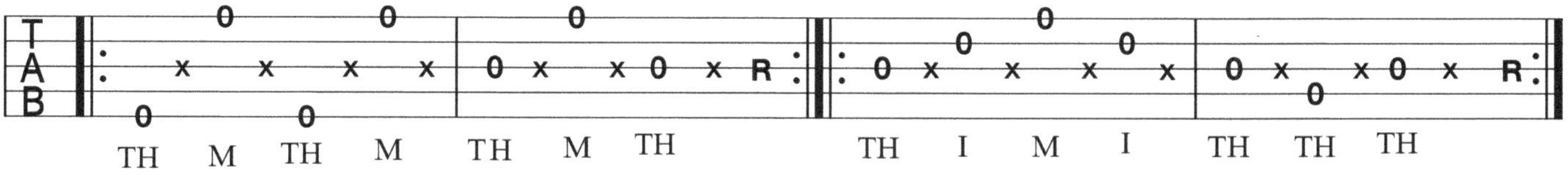

Notice all of the repeat signs. Please don't ignore them. They are there to give you the extra practice you will need to master these exercises.

It is also worth noting that as you progress through the book, not every picking finger is labeled. After a while, it is expected of you to automatically know what finger picks a particular string.

On the following page you will find more exercises to further develop your picking hand.

Picking Hand Workouts

1 (Thumb - Index)

TH I TH I · TH I TH I · TH I TH I TH I TH I · TH I TH I TH

2 (Thumb - Middle)

TH M TH M · TH M TH M · TH M TH M TH M TH M · TH M TH M TH

3 (Combo of 1 & 2)   ① "Basic Scruggs Roll" *

TH I TH M TH I TH M · TH I TH M TH I TH M · TH I TH M TH I TH M

4 (TH–I–M–TH)   (Remember: 1R = 2X)

TH I M TH · TH I M TH · TH I M TH · TH I M TH

5 (M–I–TH–M)

M I TH M · M I TH M · M I TH M · M I TH M

6 (Combo of 4 & 5)   ② "Forward-Backward Roll" *

TH I M TH M I TH M · TH I M TH M I TH M · TH I M TH M I TH M

* A "Roll" is a repeated series of picked strings, usually in 8th note groupings.
There are two banjo rolls represented on this page (see ① and ②).
Learn to play these rolls in your sleep.

THE FRETTING HAND

Four Fret Position

Figure 12 below shows how your fingers are "assigned" to each of the first four frets of the banjo. This does not mean that you hold your fingers in this position. It is just showing you how the fingers align with their "assigned" frets. This finger alignment is used primarily for playing melodies.

Each finger's full name is followed by its abbreviated name and shows how they align with the fingers and frets in the illustration.

Pinky = pink	Ring = ring	Middle = mid	Index = ind
4th fret	3rd fret	2nd fret	1st fret
any string	any string	any string	any string

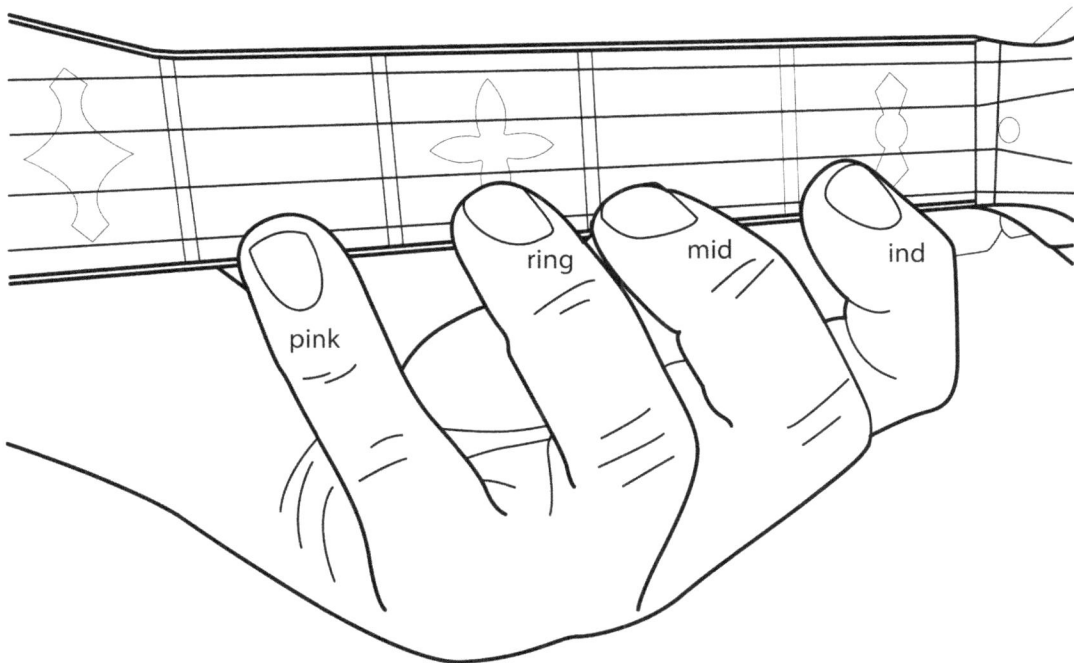

Figure 12. Four Fret Position

Fretting Hand Workouts

The finger markings appear above the tab staff to help remind you which fretting hand finger to use on a given note.

These rules may change slightly, but when that does happen you will be advised.

1 (All 1st string)

```
     open ind  mid  ring   pink ring  mid  ind    open ind  mid  ring   pink ring  mid
T  ┌──0────1────2────3────┬──4────3────2────1───┬──0────1────2────3───┬──4────3────2──────┐
A  │     x    x    x    x  │    x    x    x    x │    x    x    x    x │    x    x    x   R │
B  └──────────────────────┴────────────────────┴────────────────────┴───────────────────┘
```

M (Picks all notes)
↖ Picking hand markings are still found BELOW the Tab Staff.

2 (All 2nd string)

```
     open ind  mid  ring   pink ring  mid  ind    open ind  mid  ring   pink ring  mid
T  ┌──0────1────2────3────┬──4────3────2────1───┬──0────1────2────3───┬──4────3────2──────┐
A  │     x    x    x    x  │    x    x    x    x │    x    x    x    x │    x    x    x   R │
B  └──────────────────────┴────────────────────┴────────────────────┴───────────────────┘
```

I (Picks all notes)

3 (All 3rd string)

```
     open mid  ring  mid    open mid  open ring    open ind  mid  ring   mid  ind  open
T  ┌──0──x──2──x──3──x──2──x─┬─0──x──2──x──0──x──3──x─┬─0──x──1──x──2──x──3──x─┬─2──x──1──x──0──x──R─┐
A  │                         │                       │                       │                     │
B  └─────────────────────────┴───────────────────────┴───────────────────────┴─────────────────────┘
```

TH (Picks all notes)

This line is quite a challenge for your Pinky!

4 (All 4th string)

```
     open ind  mid  ring   pink ring  mid  ind    open mid  pink mid    pink mid  open
T  ┌─────x────x────x────x──┬───x────x────x────x──┬───x────x────x────x──┬──x────x────x───R─┐
A  │                       │                     │                     │                  │
B  └──0────1────2────3─────┴──4────3────2────1───┴──0────2────4────2───┴──4────2────0─────┘
```

TH (Picks all notes)

20

Starter Songs and Exercises

Here are some easy melodies with which you are probably familiar.

- Your successful execution of these songs relies on the abilities you have honed so far.
- Make sure you are picking the string with the correct *picking hand* finger.
- Also make sure you are fretting each given fret with the correct *fretting hand* finger.

All fingerings are marked, but that won't always be the case from here on out.

1 **Hot Cross Buns**

2 **Mary's Lamb**

3 **Brother John**

CHAPTER 5

CHORDS

This page is the beginning of forming clean-sounding chords.

New on this page:

- **Section Markers (A and B)**—Two sections of a tune that usually repeat twice each.

- **Measure Numbers**—Numbers that appear above a given measure as a place-keeper. Measures are numbered numerically from the first measure of a tune to the last. In most of the tabs' arrangements, the measure numbers appear every four measures. This tune has a total of 16 measures.

- **Short Form C Chord** (Measure 6); **D7** (Measure 15)

- **The "Pinch"**—Two strings picked simultaneously with TH and M—see Measure 16.

Fretting Fingers Workout Stage 1

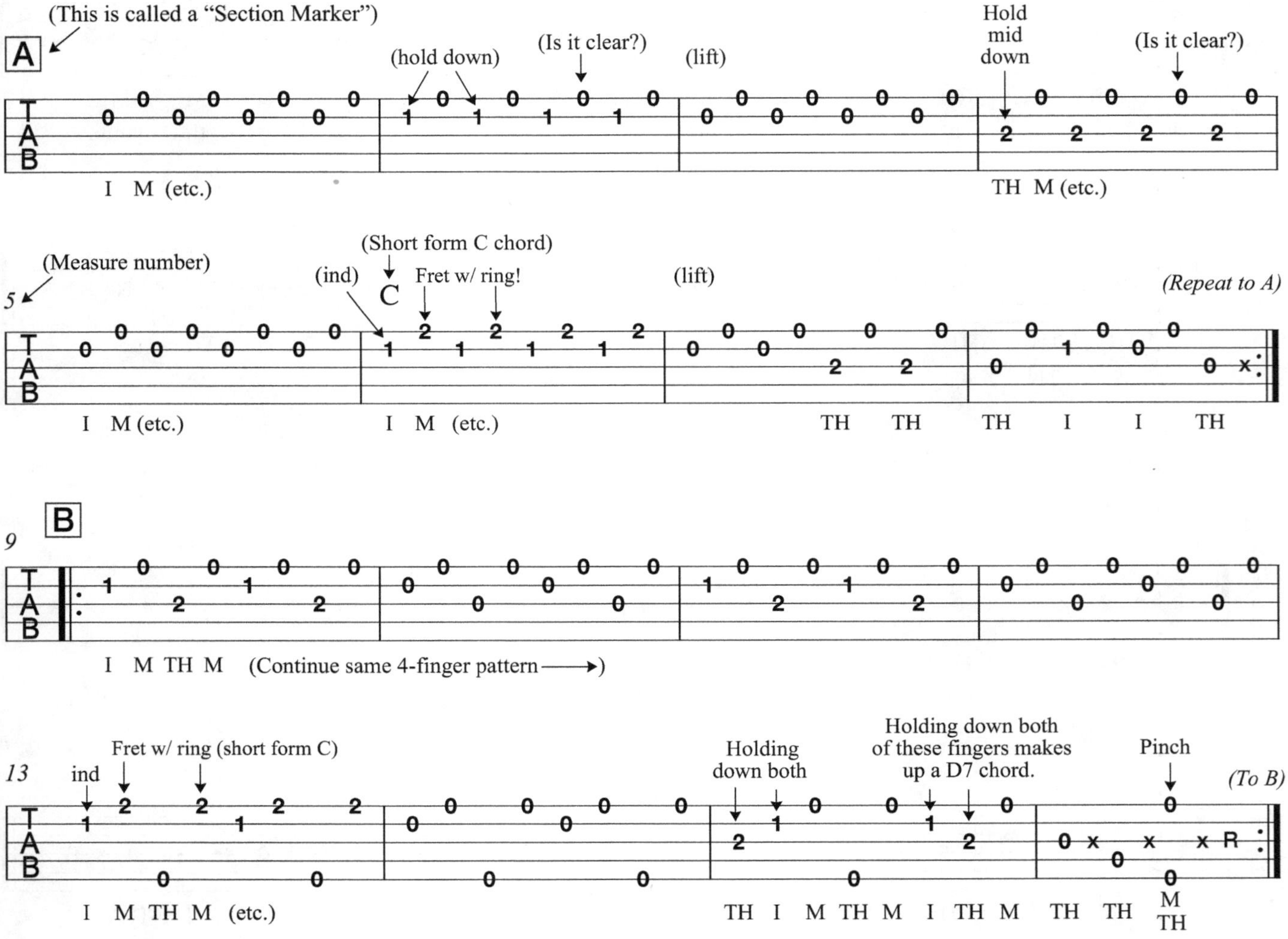

The C, D7 and D Chords

The G chord is not shown, because it is an open-string chord and doesn't require the use of the fretting hand.

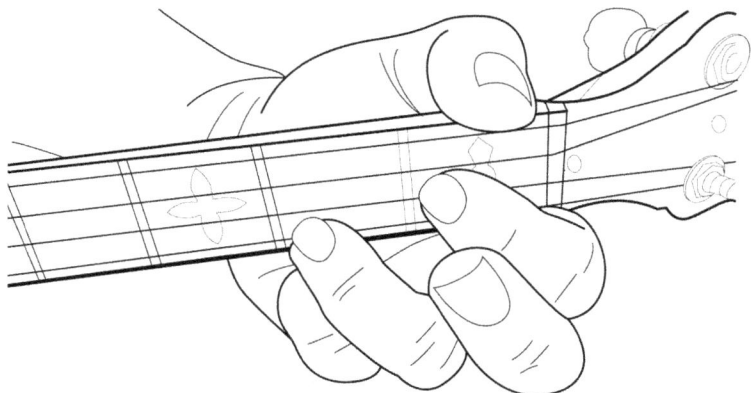

Figure 13. The C Chord

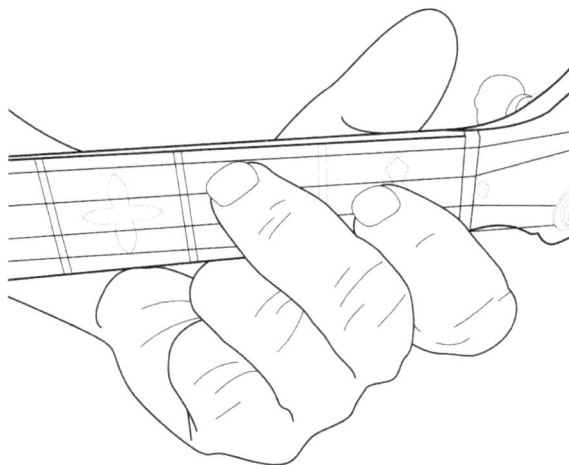

Figure 14. The D7 Chord

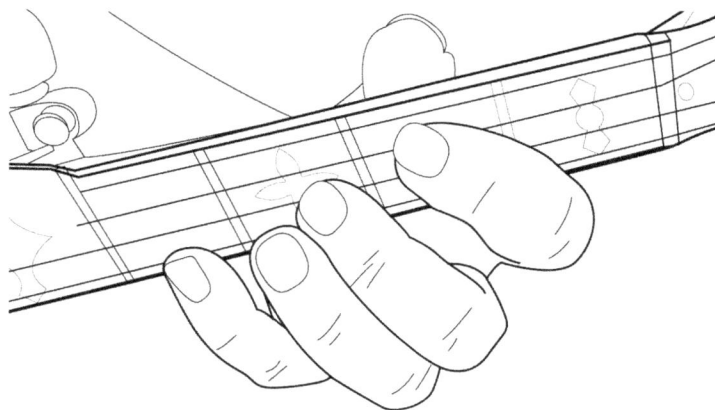

Figure 15. The D Chord

Chords and Reading Chord Diagrams

This is what your "main" four chords look like in tablature form. Try strumming the amount of strings indicated for each chord—lowest pitch to highest pitch—with the thumb (TH).

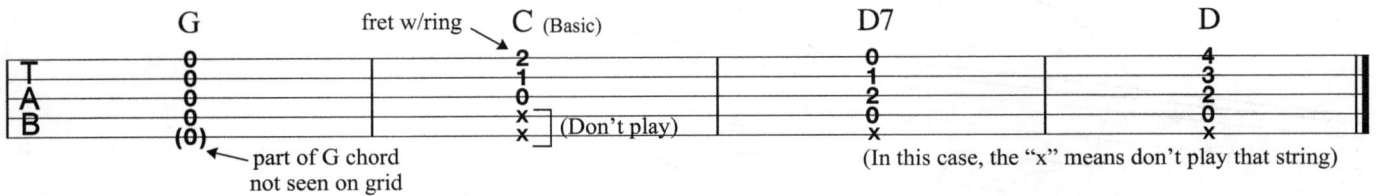

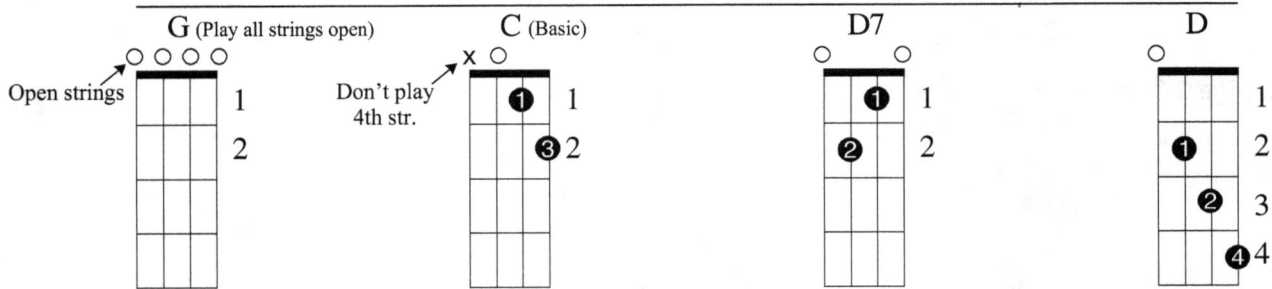

fret w/ring

part of G chord
not seen on grid

(Don't play)

(In this case, the "x" means don't play that string)

Open strings

Don't play
4th str.

About the Grid:

You are looking at the banjo as if facing it upright on a guitar stand. Therefore:

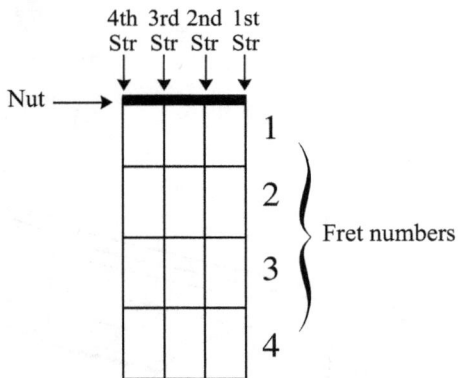

4th 3rd 2nd 1st
Str Str Str Str

Nut

Fret numbers

Sample:

The circles with the numbers in them represent the fretting hand fingers:

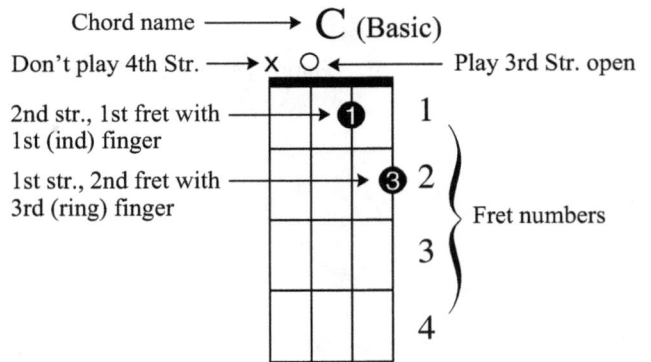

❶ ❷ ❸ ❹
ind   mid   ring   pink

Chord name ⟶ C (Basic)

Don't play 4th Str. ⟶ x ○ ⟵ Play 3rd Str. open

2nd str., 1st fret with 1st (ind) finger

1st str., 2nd fret with 3rd (ring) finger

Fret numbers

You may also come across these grids in miniature. This Basic C would look like this:

Two Basic Banjo Rolls to Practice

The top line is for practicing the pattern on the open strings. Measure 5 to the end is for practicing the pattern while changing from one chord to another.

1. Basic Scruggs Roll

TH I TH M TH I TH M   TH (etc...)   TH   TH   TH   M
                                                                                 TH

Example using the Basic Scruggs Roll

TH (Same pattern as above)

The top line is for practicing the pattern on the open strings. Measure 5 to the end is for practicing the pattern while changing from one chord to another.

2. Forward/Backward Roll

(Same) (Same) (Pinch) (Pinch)

TH I M TH M I TH M   TH I M TH (etc.)   TH   TH   M / TH   TH (On 4th!)   M / TH

Example 2. Using the Forward/Backward Roll

G   (G)   C   (C)

TH (Same as pattern above)

G   (G)   D7   (D7)

G   (G)   C   (C)

G   (G)   D (blank)   (D)

G   C   G   (G)

* I realize that trying to "land" a D chord right now seems like an impossible task. Be thankful that the D chord is not widely used in this book but keep trying to make it happen. An exercise is forthcoming to help you with the D chord.

On the next page, you will find an exercise to help you with the D chord.

Fretting Fingers Workout—Stage 2

Finger Work for that Nasty D Chord

A

(hold down)   (Is it clear?)   (lift)   mid hold down   (Is it clear?)

I   M   (etc.)

TH   M   (etc.)

5   C   fret w/ ring!   (lift)   (To A)

I   M   (etc.)

TH   TH   TH   I   I   TH

9   *   **B**   ind hold down   mid hold down   pink hold down   (D chord full form)   ind   ring   C   (C)

13   ind hold down   mid hold down   pink hold down   (D chord full form)   C   G   (To B)

17   (Ending)   ring   C   (form D chord ⟶)   ind   mid   pink   ring

* Measure 9 (or Letter B) requires a gradual placement of one finger at a time, holding each finger in place as you add them. Doing this will help train your fingers to "land" that all-elusive D chord. Also notice that the fretting hand fingers *break* the original rules that were discussed. This is necessary to make the D chord work.

A MERRY MIXTURE

(An Exercise for Timing, Chords, Rolls, and Fingering Accuracy)

By Jeff Belding

(Forward-Backward: half C, half D7)

(Half C -------- Half D7)

MELODIES TO FIVE WELL-KNOWN SONGS

In the up-coming pages, you will find the melodies for some familiar tunes.

- While learning these pieces, pay attention to the correct finger usage in both your hands.
- Also watch for the pauses.
- If something "doesn't sound right," it is usually a *rhythm* problem.
- If you like, use the four measures below as an "Intro" (Introduction) for "Ode to Joy" (up next).

M
I
TH ← Notice that 3 strings are "plucked" at once by M, I, and TH.

The songs in this section are:

1. "Ode to Joy"
2. "Long, Long Ago"
3. "Can Can" (and the G Major Scale)
4. "Simple Gifts"
5. "Camptown Races"

ODE TO JOY

Ludwig van Beethoven
Arranged by Jeff Belding

mid   ring   Look out below! *   ring   mid   ind

5   Below!

9

13   Below!

* Always be careful when reading Tabs to keep your eyes "peeled" for those 5th strings along the way—they're easy to miss!

LONG, LONG AGO

Arranged by Jeff Belding

Here is a familiar tune that is quite challenging. It makes use of the "G Major Scale" at one point in "reverse" direction. The scale is written out after the tune. After trying the scale, see if you can spot where it happens in the song.

CAN CAN (and the "G Major Scale")

Jacques Offenbach
Arranged by Jeff Belding

"G Major Scale" starting on the 3rd string, *open G*, up to 5th string, *high G* (played twice), then down again.

Do	Re	Mi	Fa	Sol	La	Ti	Do	Do	Ti	La	Sol	Fa	Mi	Re	Do
G	A	B	C	D	E	F♯*	G (high)	G (high)	F♯	E	D	C	B	A	G

* "F Sharp" (More in the future on why this is F sharp – "♯" sign means sharp.)

- Practice this scale every day. Become familiar with it. Try saying the syllables—Do, Re, Mi, Fa, Sol, La, Ti, Do—while you play it.

- Or for a real challenge, try saying the letter names as you play it.

SIMPLE GIFTS (Melody)

Traditional Shaker Hymn
Arranged by Jeff Belding

Pick-Up Notes make up an "incomplete" measure. In this case, the pick-up notes are two eighth notes. Therefore, they take up one quarter note beat so for this song just count: "1, 2, 3" then begin.

When you first hear this version of "Camptown Races," you may think, "Hey! That's not the way the song is sung!" This is a "skeletal" version of the melody—an outline of the tune. There's a "dressed up" banjo solo version in later pages.

For now, learn the melody exactly as presented, as it will become the set-up for learning that all-important *other* banjo skill known as "Accompaniment."

CAMPTOWN RACES (BASIC MELODY)

Arranged by Jeff Belding

5

9

13

(To top)

BANJO ACCOMPANIMENT

Banjo accompaniment (also known as *rhythm* banjo) should become an integral part of your playing. *One of the goals in this series is to give you the ability to go out into the "field of pickers," and be able to play right along with them as either an accompanist or a soloist.*

The version of rhythm banjo presented here is not the typical-sounding accompaniment that you might hear on your favorite bluegrass recordings. It is presented in this simplified approach for two main reasons:

- It will help you to understand the chord structure of a song.
- It will make it easier for you to "join in with the band" and play along with relative ease using the basic chords that you already know.

More advanced accompaniment techniques are covered in future volumes of this series.

The following are some exercises (A–D) to prepare you for the accompaniment to "Camptown Races" and a myriad of other tunes in four/quarter time (four/quarter (4/4) time is: Four quarter-note beats, or eight eighth-note beats in a measure).

Preparatory Exercise for Banjo Accompaniment

Remember when playing accompaniment, you are in a supportive role, play quietly.

Camptown Races

Basic Banjo Accompaniment in Four/Quarter Time

The lyrics to a song are normally written below the staff. Due to other markings you will find where the lyrics align with the accompaniment above the staff.

Camp - town   la - dies   sing   this   song.   Do - dah.   Do - dah.

G   D7   (D7)

TH   M   TH   M   (etc.)
   I   I

* Practice 1st measure over and over.

Camp - town   race   track   five   miles   long.   Oh,_____   do - dah   day.

5   G   D7   G

Gon - na   run   all   night;   gon - na   run   all   day.   I

9   (G)   C   ←— ring*   G

add
mid

bet   my   money   on   the   bob - tail   nag,   some - body   bet   on   the   bay.

13   (G)   D7   G   (Back to top)

*   With your C chord accompaniment, be absolutely sure to play the C chord with the ring finger on the 1st string/2nd fret.

NEW FRETTING HAND TECHNIQUES AND THEIR USES IN EXERCISES AND SOLOS

Higher Notes and "Barring" Exercise

The banjo tune on the next page was written for the purpose of teaching you two new fingering techniques:

1. Reaching higher up the neck for some commonly-used notes—referred to as the *"9/10" position* (see Measure 2 and illustration below).

2. *Barring* (see Measure 3 and illustration below): Your index finger is in for a rude awakening of what it must do. Most of you will find that your first 50 or more attempts to a clean-sounding barre position (abbreviated "Bar" in the tablature) will be met with frustration. If it sounds less than stellar right now, just try to roll with it. With some slight experimentation of moving the barring finger around a little here and there, you will eventually find the "sweet spot." Use your thumb from behind the banjo neck as a clamp to help hold that barre down. Your barring strength will develop over time, so be patient with a barre that for now may sound more like a thud than a nice musical combination of notes. For barring, flatten your (preferably) index finger over the 1st, 2nd and 3rd strings at the fret that is called for. Some barres call for barring all four "main" strings or even sometimes all five but start with three for now.

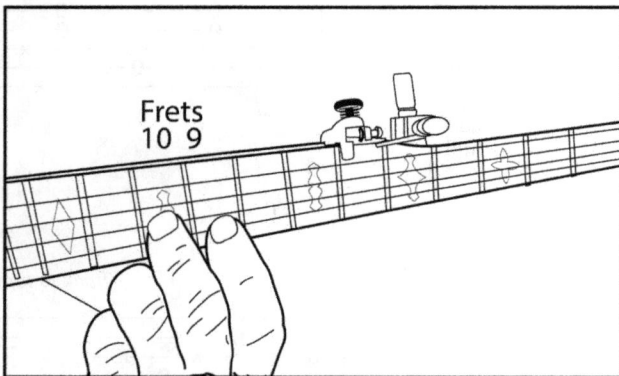

Figure 16. The 9/10 Position

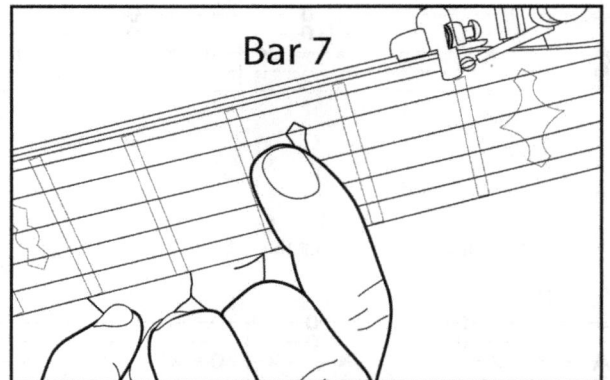

Figure 17. The Barre Position

This example of the Barre position (Figure 17) shows the index finger at the 7th fret.

For Barre 5, simply move the index finger back two frets to the 5th fret.

Higher Notes and "Barring" Exercise

By Jeff Belding

This is not really a chord. It's referred to as a "single-finger position." (Two fingers down simultaneously)

"9/10" position

Bar 7th fret

single finger position

(Repeat to A)

Barre 5th fret

Barre 7th fret

fret w/ind.

Barre 5th fret **

"9/10 position"

Barre 7th fret *

fret w/ind.

(Repeat to B)

** The barre at 5th fret is a type of C chord.

* The barre at 7th fret is a type of D chord.

A Study of an Irish Jig—"Irish Washerwoman" in 3/8 Time

For this tune, "Irish Washerwoman," you will be counting measures in groups of three:
1 - 2 - 3 - 1 - 2 - 3, and so on. The only exception is the first measure with just two pick-up notes.

This is a good time to continue explaining how to "count off" a song, especially when you're playing with a group of two or more people. For songs in four/quarter time, you count "1 - 2 - 3 - 4" and then begin. For songs with three beats to a measure like this one, you would count "1 - 2 - 3" and then begin. The problem with this scenario, is that this song has an "incomplete measure" at the beginning with two pick-up notes.

The formula for figuring out how to count off this tune (or any tune) the *right* way is as follows: Take the number of beats per measure (in this case three), subtract the number of pick-up beats (in this case, two) and you come up with one. You can't count off a song effectively by just saying "1." So, you count one full measure of three plus an extra one— "1 - 2 - 3 - 1," then play. This formula works the same when in four/quarter time. The chart below may help you.

Song	Beats per Measure	No. of Pick-up Notes	Do the Math	The Count Off
Cripple Creek	4	1	4 – 1 = 3	1–2–3
Red River Valley	4	2	4 – 2 = 2	1–2–3–4–1–2*
Home on the Range	3	1	3 – 1 = 2	1–2–3–1–2 (best)
When the Saints Go Marching In	4	3	4 – 3 = 1	1 (too short) therefore: 1–2–3–4–1

* Counting just "1–2" doesn't allow much lead time, so a full measure of 4 followed by 1-2 is the best way to handle it.

IRISH WASHERWOMAN (Melody)

Arranged by Jeff Belding

(2nd time, remember to skip to "2.")

15

1.
2.
(Remember the "9/10 position?")
mid [B] ind
(lift)

TH   TH   I   M

20   ind   9/10 pos.   mid   barre 7th fret

25   (Shift back)   ind→

31   1.   *(To B)*   2.   (Ending – "Tag")   C   G
mid
M   M
I   I

37   D7   G   Back-strum
(1st to 5th w/ I)
I   I
TH   TH   I

The Irish Washerwoman accompaniment on the following page is in "three/eighth" time—indicating there are three eighth-note beats in a measure. The first beat of a measure is picked on the 3rd string with the thumb (of the picking hand). The second two beats of a measure are plucked on the 2nd and 1st strings simultaneously by the index and middle fingers. This pattern is the same for every measure until Measure 16, when there is a pause of two eighth-note beats. There is a similar pause in Measure 32. Then in Measure 33, there is a new pattern of three string plucks using all three picking hand fingers.

There is a *new chord:* A minor ("Amin"). This "Amin" chord occurs in Measures 27 and 35. The small diagram above Measure 27 helps you to figure out the fingering. For more information on Amin, see a larger scale diagram at the end of the piece.

IRISH WASHERWOMAN (Accompaniment in 3/8 Time)

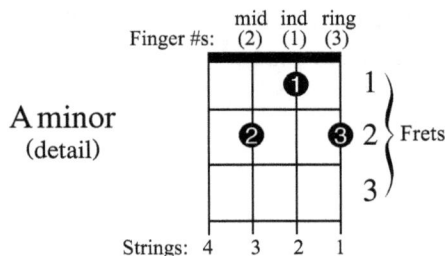

40

Non-Picking Maneuvers

Hammer-ons (h) Pull-offs (P) Slides (sl)

A "non-picking maneuver" is the act of producing two or more notes with a single stroke of the pick.

1. Hammer-ons (marked with a lower case "h")

Look at Measure 1. The idea here is to pick the 4th string open (with TH) and *hammer-on* ("slam down") your middle finger (of the fretting hand) onto the 4th string/2nd fret. There is the temptation to pick the string again, but you must trust your fretting hand to do the work for that second note with absolutely no help from the picking hand. Chances are on your first few tries at this, you will get very little sound (if any) out of that second note. That is why *every* measure in this series of exercises has a repeat sign.

You will need *many* repetitions to make this sound worthwhile. However, don't spend an hour on your first time doing this hammer-on maneuver. Take just two minutes (even set a timer) and work on Measure 1. Then, practice something else to get away from it for 10 minutes or so. By practicing these non-picking maneuvers in small concentrated segments of time, you will build up your fretting hand strength, gradually gaining a useful callous rather than a painful blister.

1 Hammer-on's (h)

2. Pull-offs (marked with a "P")

A *pull-off* is the opposite maneuver from a hammer-on. Look at Measure 9. The idea is to pick the note (with TH) at the 4th string/2nd fret and then pull that middle finger downward and to the side. You are literally picking the string with your fretting hand middle finger in order to get the open 4th string to sound, without help from the picking hand.

2 Pull-off's (P)

Keep in mind that a *pull-off* is not the lifting of the fretting hand finger. A mere lift would not give you enough sound. Once again, practice these in small one- or two-minute segments, then go work on something else. This will build up your finger strength gradually.

3. **Slides** (Marked "sl")

Look at Measure 17 below. In this case, the *slide* is executed with the middle finger of the fretting hand moving along (or "sliding") from 3rd string/2nd fret to 3rd string/4th fret. The TH of the picking hand picks (in this case) the 3rd string/2nd fret (fretted with middle) and then the middle finger slides to the 4th fret of the 3rd string, without another stroke of the picking hand. There is a fine line between too much pressure on the sliding finger and not enough pressure. You have your starting fret and then you have your "target" fret. The goal is for only those two notes to sound, while any frets in-between are not really heard. From behind the neck, your thumb (of the fretting hand) should move like a "lever" rotating almost 90 degrees. If the thumb stays at the same angle, the slide will both feel and sound cumbersome.

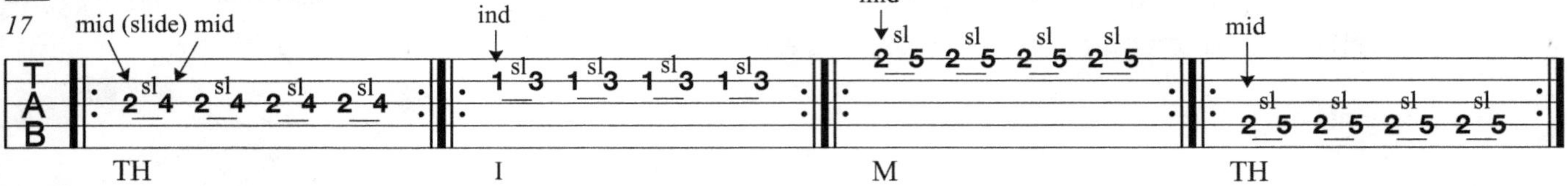

From here on, you will be encountering these various non-picking maneuvers. There are some other finger and fret variations. If you have a good command of all of these previous exercises, you will be able to tackle most any one that comes along. There are also some "rhythmic" variations, which will be explained in more detail as they occur.

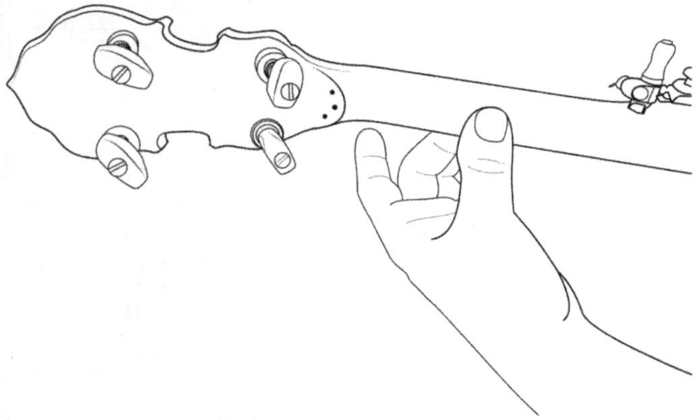

Figure 18. Slide Preparation

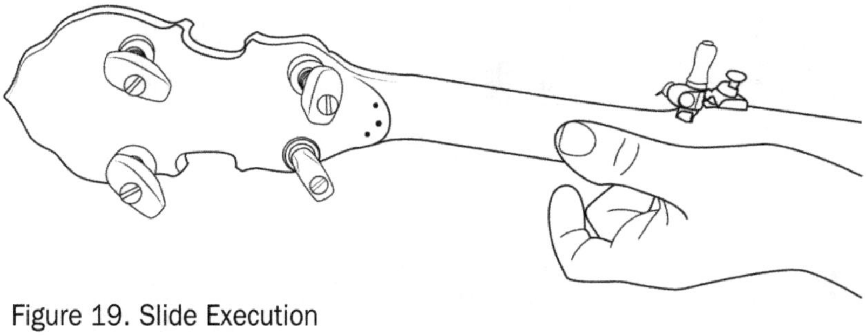

This pair of diagrams shows you what happens with the thumb behind the neck when executing a smooth slide.

Figure 19. Slide Execution

New Terms, Concepts, Markings and Fretting Antics

(Useful knowledge to have before going forward)

A **The "Walk-Up"**—This is a series of (usually) quarter notes that act as a "bridge" to lead you back to the beginning of a song, or lead you into the ending of the song.

B **Basic Scruggs Roll with alternating Thumb (of the Picking Hand)**—TH picks the 3rd string at the start of the first four notes. TH picks the 4th string at the start of the *second* group of four notes.

C **Lick* with built-in Pull-off.**

D **16th notes**—Two 16th notes fit into the space of one 8th note. Therefore, they are twice as fast as the 8th notes in a measure. They almost always appear in some kind of *non-picking maneuver* (e.g., "sl"). You will find your first marking for a pair of 16th notes at the beginning of Measure D. The "peak-shaped" bracket denotes the pair of 16th notes.

TH I TH M TH I TH M

E **"G Run"**—Another "bridge" measure, similar to a Walk-up.

F **Measure with 16th-note Hammer-on** ("h").

G **"G Fill #1"**—You will be seeing this measure quite often from here on. It provides a "filler" between sections of a tune.

H **3-String Pinch**—A little more challenging than the standard "pinch," but should be self-explanatory.

TH   TH I   M   I TH M   TH   TH   M
                                              I
                                             TH

* **"What is a lick?"**— It is a series of the same notes that may appear several times at various parts of a song. You will find the long answer in *Appendix C*.

The "8X" Pages—Part 1

(Part 2 to follow later on)

Play each of the following exercises 8 times ("X").

1 G – Forward/Backward

2 Basic Scruggs w/ alternating thumb

3 Two Basic Scruggs Rolls per measure

4 More Basic Scruggs variations

5 G Fill #1

Banjo Exercise I

(Use of Rolls, Licks and Non-Picks)

By Jeff Belding

Camptown Races—Banjo Solo

When you first hear this solo version of "Camptown Races," you may think, "Hey! I don't hear the melody that much." Taking a familiar song like "Camptown Races" and presenting it as a banjo solo requires some changes to the song's basic melody. The following are some examples of how this was done for this solo:

- Look at the last two notes of Measure 1 going into the first six notes of Measure 2. The melody is found on the 1st and 2nd strings. The 5th string notes that occur between those melody notes are additions or "filler." They give the song a new vibrancy, and a driving rhythm that is *so* characteristic of the 5-string banjo sound.

- Now look at Measure 7. Some of the melody notes were removed ("subtracted") and replaced with a forward-backward roll on a D7 chord. In this measure, the melody is "implied" rather than stated "note for note."

Please obey the pauses (Xs). The spaces between the notes are *just* as important as the notes themselves.

("Rocking") * ... D7

5 — _("Rocking")_ — D7 (Forward-Backward) — (G Fill #1)

9 — C — G

13 — D7 (Forward-Backward) — (To Top)

* **Rocking**—A technique that involves the repetitious motion of two fingers of the picking hand several times in a row. In this song, the rocking occurs from M to TH several times. More details to come.

Measures 8 and 9 may be challenging. Reviewing the "Non-Picking Maneuvers," the "8X" pages and "Banjo Exercise I" should be helpful.

CHAPTER 9

BANJO IMITATO, CHORD PROGRESSIONS AND A SNEAK PEEK AT HOW TO IMPROVISE

Banjo Imitato (Teacher plays Exercise, Student Imitates it Back)

To hear how Banjo Imitato works refer to the Audio download. These exercises serve two main purposes:

1. Technique – On the surface, they are exercises to improve your technical abilities.

2. Improvising – Each numbered exercise has a chord name written above it to show you its intended use with that chord for creating an improvised solo. More details on this as you work your way through this chapter.

Exercise 1 — G — (G – Forward/Backward)

Exercise 2 — G — Your first time doing a hammer-on *starting* with a fretted note.

Exercise 3 — C — (C chord down throughout)

Exercise 4 — C — (C chord down throughout) / (C chord acrobatics!) *

Exercise 5 — G — (Similar to ②, 3rd ms.)

* To play the third measure of "Exercise 4," you *must* fret the 1st string/2nd fret (of the C chord) with your ring finger!

G

⑥

```
T  |:----0----5----5----5----5--|--5----0--------------0--|--2^h3---0----------0--|--0-------0--x--x----0--:|
A  |:-5--------------------------|-----------0--x--x------|------------------2----|--------0^h2-------------|
B  |:-0-------0-------0----------|--0---------------0-----|--0---------0----------|-----------------0------|
```
↑
Heads up!

M
TH

D7

⑦ D7   Off D7   D7 down   (Unusual fingering)
                                                                                           Fret w/   ind
                                                                                           ring

```
T  |:----0----0---------0----0--|--2^h3----3----0----0--|--0--------0----0----0--|------------------0--------|
A  |:-2-------1---------1-------|--x--------------------|-----1----1----1-------|-----0--2 sl 4----2--x--R--:|
B  |:-0-----------------0-------|--0-------------0----0--|--2-------2----2----2---|---------------------------|
```
                                                       TH   TH   TH M

D7

⑧   D7   (Still D7)   "Rocking" *

```
T  |:----0----0--2^h3---0--------0--|--0----0----1----0--|--0----0----0----0--|--0----0----0----------|
A  |:-0--x--x--x-----------------3--|--3---------2-------|-----1----1--------|-----------------x-----|
B  |:-0-----------------0---------0-|--0---------0-------|--2-------2----2----|--0--2--4--0-----------|
```
                                                                              TH TH TH TH

G

⑨   "Rocking"   G fill #1

```
T  |:----0--2^h3---0----0--------0--|--0----0----0----0--|--0----5----0------0--|--0----------0--------|
A  |:-0-------------------2---------|--0-----------------|--0--x-------2------|--0--x--x--0--R--:|
B  |:-0-----------0-----------------|--2----0----2------|--0----------------|--0----0---------|
```
                                                                              M
                                                                              I
                                                                              TH

* **"Rocking"** (originally used in "Camptown Races") is a useful banjo technique that will soon be covered in more detail.

How to Use the Stuff from Banjo Imitato for Improvising

What is a chord progression? It is a series of two or more chords that *progress* from one to the next in a logical fashion for a predetermined amount of measures. When the cycle of chords is complete, then it may start over again, or a new one may be introduced. A chord progression is what gives a song its structure.

One might think every song has its own unique chord progression, but songs with different melodies can have the same progression. If you can play the accompaniment for the chord progression on the following page, you have the ability to play rhythm banjo for many songs.

This particular progression is fairly easy to follow, because it is quite symmetrical:

Two measures of G, progressing to two measures of C, progressing to two measures of D7, progressing to two measures of G—then starting back over on the first measure of G again.

Now try playing it through:

G   (G)   C   mid   (C)   mid

(tablature)

5   D7   (D7)   G   (G)

(tablature)

In a bluegrass jam, your initial role in this hypothetical song would be to play this accompaniment over and over. A typical bluegrass song consists of a verse followed by a chorus and then an instrumental solo. You can continue on the same accompaniment through such a structure – *but* eventually someone will look at you and say, "Take it!" (meaning time for *your* solo!) Then what do you do?

You can take the licks and rolls that you have learned over time and *plug them in* at the "right measure," that goes with the "right chord." The licks on the "Banjo Imitato" pages can be pieced together to create such a solo. Here is an example of how to do this.

To start with, I need 2 measures of something to go with a G chord: *Then, I need 2 measures of something to go with a C chord:*

9   G   C   (C)

(tablature)

⟵ (Banjo Imitato – ① 1st 2 measures) ⟶   ⟵ (Banjo Imitato – ③ 1st 2 measures) ⟶

Next, I need 2 measures of something to go with a D7 chord: *And now, I need 2 measures back on a G chord:*

13   D7

(tablature)

⟵ (Banjo Imitato – ⑧ 3rd and 4th measures) ⟶   ⟵ (Banjo Imitato – ⑤ 1st 2 measures) ⟶

At this point, the solo is only half over, since the chord progression is repeated twice to complete a cycle. You could play it safe and repeat everything you just did two times or…you could go on and cherry-pick more licks for the next eight measures of the solo. On the following page is an example.

17   ⟵ (2 measures of G Chord "Stuff") ⟶   C   (C)

```
T  | 0       0   0    | 0      0        | 2   2   2  | 2   2     2  |
A  |0 x 2h3      2    | 5   0     0  x  x|1 1   1   1 |1   1     1   |
B  |              0   |0        0       |  0   0     |   0      0    |
```

(Banjo Imitato – ⑤ 3rd measure)   (Banjo Imitato – ⑥ 2nd measure)   ⟵ (Banjo Imitato – ④ 1st 2 measures) ⟶

21   D7   (D7)   ring   ⟵ (2 measures of G Chord "Stuff") ⟶

```
T  |0    0   0  |0    0   0    |0    0   | 0      0     |
A  | 1 1 1  1 1 | 1 1 | 1   1  |5  5 5 5|5  0          |
B  | 2    2    |0   2    2     | 0     0|  0    0 x  x  |
```

(Banjo Imitato – ⑦ 3rd measure)   (Banjo Imitato – ⑧ 3rd measure)   ⟵ (Banjo Imitato – ⑥ 1st 2 measures) ⟶

In the "real world" of bluegrass, you would return to measure 1 on the previous page. Thus, going back to playing "rhythm banjo," while the singer sings a verse, or another instrumentalist takes a solo.

These licks and phrases could be rearranged in other orders. And you'll get a whole different and interesting solo out of them. It takes a little experimentation, because some phrases transfer well next to each other, whereas other combinations might sound awkward. It's also a matter of whether the picking hand works smoothly or not when combining certain phrases. *And*, please be aware that you are not limited to the phrases from "Banjo Imitato." Anything that you have picked up along the way from other exercises is fair game for use in your personal creation of a solo.

Like this chord progression, any chord progression of a song can be broken down into a "block diagram" (measure to measure) format of its structure.

Here is what your current chord progression looks like in this form:

```
‖: G    | G    | C    | C    |
  | D7   | D7   | G    | G    :‖
```

Don't be too concerned if these past three pages have left you scratching your head in wonderment. If you don't understand any of it, just take the time to learn the sample solo starting on the previous page (Measures 9 through 24). This is a little "peek" inside of the door to that daunting world of "music theory," which you'll re-visit in later volumes in this series.

The nice thing about that chord progression in its block diagram form, is it gives you a lot of information to work with in a short-hand version. This is what most musicians refer to as a "chord chart."

By looking at this "chord chart," you can know how to play accompaniment without having to read all of those "picks and plucks" found on top of the previous page of this section back at measure 1.

Chord charts for most all the songs in this book are available for download from my website, musicalongtheway.com. The charts available are listed in *Appendix A*. That way, if you know a guitarist who can play pretty solid bluegrass rhythm guitar, then that person could be coerced (or bribed) into playing rhythm for the tunes and songs you have been working on in this book.

CHAPTER 10

TWO SONGS/TWO TIME SIGNATURES

Home on the Range—Banjo Melody

Waltz—3/4 Time (say "three-quarter" time)

This is your first waltz which is in 3/4 (three quarter) time. Up to now, most of your songs have been in 4/4 time. When you see a "time signature" (such as 4/4, 3/4, 3/8) call it by its full name. For example, when you see "4/4", instead of saying "four-four"—call it "four quarter" time. That way, you are acknowledging that there are four quarter notes in a measure, or the equivalent in eight eighth notes. 3/4 (three quarter) time has three quarter notes in a measure, or the equivalent in six eighth notes.

There is also one pick-up note on the first word, "Oh." Refer to your "Count Off Chart" on the first page of the "Irish Washerwoman" (page 38) to see how to count the song off.

What may seem like a simple song to sing, you will find to be quite a challenge to play. The combination of notes versus pauses is not easy to digest at first. This tune is also included to help you work your pinky as you try to nail all of those 4th string/4th frets.

Good luck, Cowpokes!

HOME ON THE RANGE (Banjo Melody)

Arranged by Jeff Belding

Oh, give me a home where the buf - fa - lo

roam, where the deer and the an - te - lope play.

Where sel - dom is heard a dis - cour - ag - ing

word, and the skies are not cloud - y all day.

16

Home,   home   on   the   range,

20

where   the   deer   and   the   an - te - lope   play.

24

Where   sel - dom   is   heard   a   dis - cour - ag - ing

28

word,   and   the   skies   are   not   cloud - y   all

31 *

C   D7

day.

* You could say that measures 31, 32, and 33 are "6-Note" banjo rolls. Down the line, these will come in useful as licks for Waltz-Style Soloing.

Home on the Range (Accompaniment in 3/4 Time)

The accompaniment for "Home on the Range" is quite similar to that of "The Irish Washerwoman." Visually, the only differences for this song are the pauses (Xs) between the notes in a measure. That is because this song uses quarter-note accompaniment, versus eighth-note accompaniment for "The Irish Washerwoman."

This song is a ballad, so it is played fairly slowly, whereas "Irish Washerwoman" is a jig and moves along at a faster pace.

HOME ON THE RANGE (Accompaniment in 3/4 Time)

Arranged by Jeff Belding

* To play the "A" Chord—barre the 2nd fret on the 3rd, 2nd, and 1st strings.

In the not-too-distant future, you'll be able to just look at a series of chords and know the necessary accompaniment to play for the song at hand, without the need for reading tablature.

On the Audio, you will find a version of "Home on the Range" with both parts together on two banjos.

Oh! Susanna (Banjo Melody in 4/4 Time)

Arranged by Jeff Belding

Oh, I've come from Al - a bam - a with my ban - jo on my

knee. I am going to Loui - si - an - a, there my true love for to

see. Oh! Su - san - na, oh don't you cry for me, for I

come from Al - a - bam - a with the ban - jo on my knee. *(Oh, I've)*

Ending   Learn this famous "tag-ending!"

Shave and a hair - cut, two bits.

Watch out for:

- The double notes in measures 1, 5, and 13.
- The timing of the *pull-off* at the end of measures 1, 5, and 13.
- The *pairs* of 8th rests (x x) in measures 1, 5, and 13.
- The slides in measures 3, 7, and 15.
- The *pinch-slide* combination in measure 19.

OH! SUSANNA (Banjo Solo)

Arranged by Jeff Belding

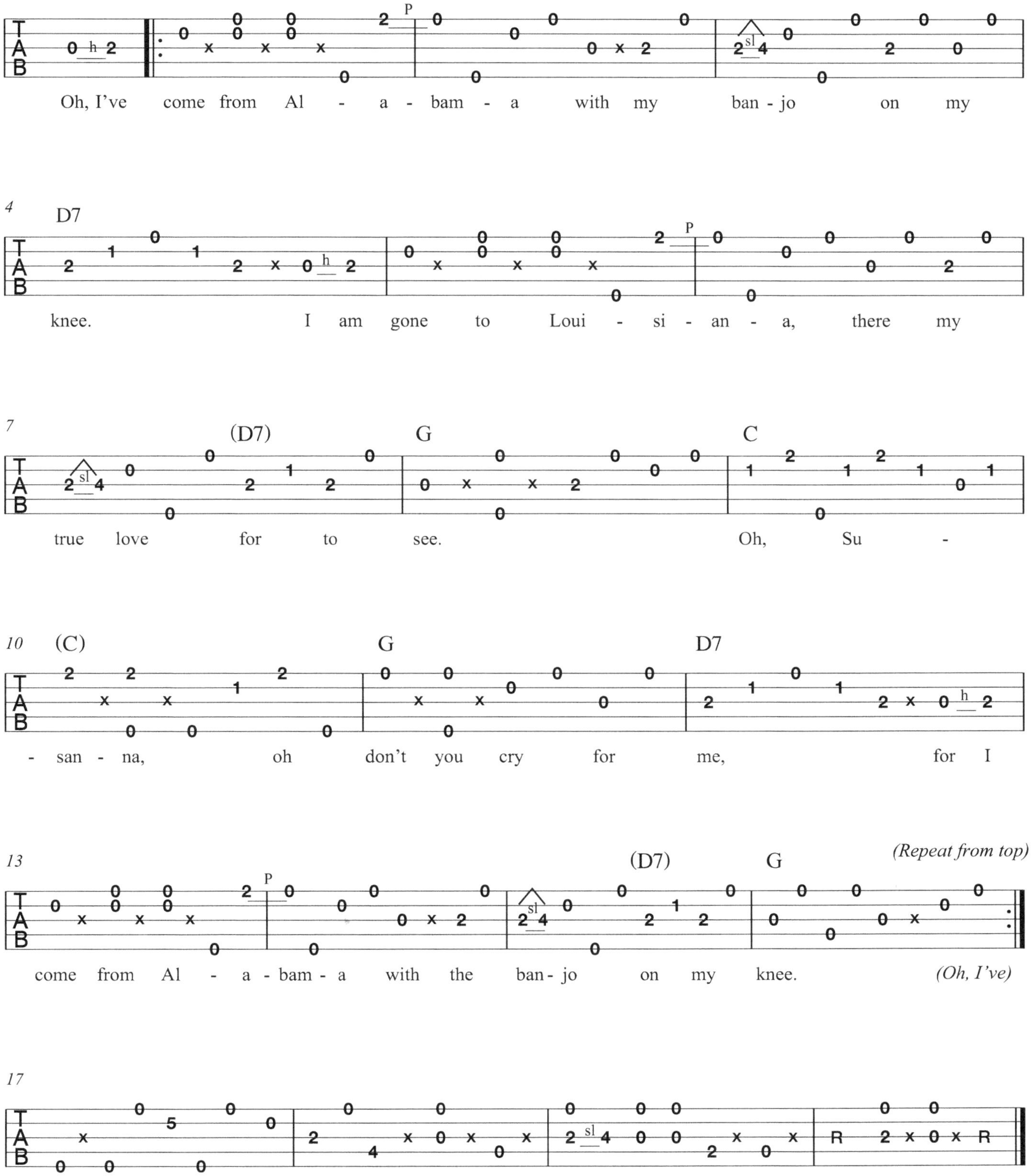

EXPLORING THE "ROCKING" TECHNIQUE

Banjo Exercise II—Examples of "Rocking" Found in Measures 3, 5, 8, 9, and 10

Reach pink

4

8

12

15   Forewad-Backward Roll

ring

Ending
(To Top)

* Remember not to rush your eighth-note hammer-ons, pull-offs, and slides.

TH   I   TH
(Try this picking.)

Shortnin' Bread—Part One (Warm-Up Exercises)

On our next page are some new techniques before tackling "Shortnin' Bread." The first is to have your picking hand index (I) finger pick the 3rd string. Until now, the Index has been assigned to the 2nd string and the TH to the 3rd string. However, when skipping from the 3rd to the 5th string, the Index *now* picks the 3rd followed by TH picking 5th, thus an effortless "string-skipping" flow.

Start with the following exercise and notice this *new* use of the index finger:

A

```
T |--0--x-----x--0--x-----x--|--0--x-----x--0--x-----x--:||--x--0--x-----x--0--x--|--x--0--x-----x--0--x--:|
A |-------------------------|-------------------------||-----------------------|----------------------|
B |-----0--------0----------|-----0--------0----------||-----0--------0--------|-----0--------0-------|
     I  TH  I  TH   I  TH   I  TH    TH  I  TH  I  TH  I  TH
   (On 3rd!)
```

That was quarter-note timing. Now try the next similar exercise in primarily eighth-note timing.

B

```
T |--0--0--0--0--|--0--0--0--0--x--:||--0--0--0--0--|--0--0--0--x--:|
A |--------------|---------------- ||--------------|--------------|
B |--0--0--0--0--|--0--0--0--0-----||--0--0--0--0--|--0--0--0-----|
     I TH I TH (etc.)        TH I      TH I TH I (etc.)       I TH
```

Having played Exercise B, you should now see the importance of using the separate fingers to pick the 3rd and 5th string. If you tried the same exercise using just your thumb (TH), you would find it very awkward to "jump over" that 4th string smoothly. However, other than this situation, you should continue to follow the picking finger rules as originally laid down. You will always get a "head's-up" when the usual rules are altered.

The next exercise involves some fancy acrobatics at the 5th Fret:

C — Start with your pinky fretting the 1st string, 5th fret: / Then add your ring finger at the 2nd string, 5th fret: / Now, pluck both together: / Now, picking separately:

```
       pink                    ring
T |--5--5--5--5--|--5--5--5--5--|--5--5--5--5--|--5--5--5--5--|
A |--x--x--x--x--|--5--x--5--x--5--x--5--x--|--5--5--5--5--x--|
B |              |              |  x  x  x  x    |            x |
```

And now, Exercise D uses the previous fingering to play a section of "Shortnin' Bread":

D

```
   (Start)         lift              lift              lift
    pink  ring  ↓         pink ring  ↓        pink ring  ↓
T ||--5-----0--0--|--5-----0--0--|--5-----0--2--|--0--0-----0--|
A |:-----5--x--x--|-----5--x--x--|-----5--------|--------2--0--x--x--:|
B ||--0--0-----0--|--0--0-----0--|--0--0-----0--|-----------0--------|
```

Now try the actual tune on the next page…

Shortnin' Bread—Part Two (Pickin' the Tune)

Arranged by Jeff Belding

Banjo "Rocking" Exercise (Wide use of TH to M, Some I to M)

Here is a fun tune based on some of the techniques you've learned over the last few pages:

(This is the trickiest part!)

Ending

RED RIVER VALLEY (Basic Melody)

Arranged by Jeff Belding

(Re: Audio—After 4-count, wait for the guitar "strum" before coming in.)

(Rests are still good on repeat.)

From this val - ley they say you are go - ing.

5

We will miss your bright eyes and sweet smile.

9

For they say you are tak - ing the sun - shine,

1. (To top)

13

that has bright - ened my path - way a while.

Ending

17 2. C D7 G

while.

RED RIVER VALLEY (Banjo Solo)

Arranged by Jeff Belding

(Re: Audio—For this version, come in *immediately* after the 4-count)

From this val - ley they say you are go - ing.

We will miss your bright eyes and sweet smile.

For they say you are tak - ing the sun - shine,

that has bright - ened my path - way a while.

while.

REVISITING THE "G MAJOR SCALE" / GARRY OWEN

Here's the G major scale from back on the "Can Can" page, coming back to visit. Play it again and focus particularly on the third and fourth measures (Do, Ti, La, Sol, Fa, Mi, Re, Do). These eight notes in reverse order (high pitch to low pitch) occur three times during the A section of "Garry Owen." In fact, the first eight notes from the beginning of the tune are taken right out of the third and fourth measure of the "G Major Scale Exercise." You will also find a familiar fingering (in the B part) at the 9th and 10th frets that was used in the "Irish Washerwoman," so playing that tune again will no doubt help you execute this tune.

Both "Garry Owen" and "Irish Washerwoman" are also Irish jigs and therefore share the same time signature (3/8, or three eighth notes per measure).

G major scale starting on 3rd string/open G up to 5th string/high G (played twice), then down again.

* "F sharp" (More in the the future on why this is F sharp.)

- Practice this scale every day. Become familiar with it. Try saying the syllables (Do, Re, Mi, Fa, Sol, La, Ti, Do) while you play it.

- Or for a real challenge, try saying the letter names as you play them.

Here is one final exercise to prepare you for "Garry Owen." This is in 4/4 time, but it sets you up well for some of the important fretting hand positions, including that all-important shift to the 10th fret "area" ("9-10" position").

GARRY OWEN (Melody)

Arranged by Jeff Belding

* Try this unusual fingering It may smooth it out.

* For a smooth transition from measures 36-37, slide your ring finger from 9th fret to 5th fret, remaining lightly in contact with the 1st string.

Garry Owen Accompaniment in 3/8 Time

Here is the accompaniment for "Garry Owen." It is in "three-eighth" time—that is three eighth-note beats in a measure. The first beat of a measure is picked on the 3rd string with the thumb (of the picking hand). The second two beats of a measure are plucked on the 2nd and 1st strings simultaneously by your index and middle fingers. This pattern is the same for most of the tune, but there are some pauses where it seemed appropriate to work well with the melody.

You will also find a different approach to the "usual" three-beat accompaniment at the first eight measures of the B section. Again, this is a good approach for being in that supportive role to the melody.

At the ending, are a couple of "challenging chords" (Measures 34, 35 and 36). They add some nice harmony to the melody part. If they are too much trouble, you can "get away with" strumming all open G chords instead. Listen for two pick-up notes in the melody before you begin!

B Tricky rhythm!

17 G

21 C

25 G

Skip 2nd time. → **1.** *(To B)*

29 D7 (D7) (Pause)

Ending

2.

33 G   G ("D shape") *   (High G barre)   G ("D shape")

* The "G-D shape" chord is a type of G chord higher up the neck. If you know your regular D chord (frets 2, 3, & 4), it is just a matter of placing the same finger combination at frets 7, 8, & 9 (same strings). There is of course a "theoretical" explanation of why that is the case and will be explained in future volumes. The high G bar should be self-explanatory as to what you need to do.

Some Practice Tips

Let's say you want to practice one hour per day. If you can make that commitment, you *will* make good progress. Now, let's map out your hour:

Preparation: Set a timer for one hour and ten minutes. This gives you ten minutes to get set up, get your practice materials ready and get your instrument in tune.

Warm-up: Spend five to eight minutes playing stuff that you *really* enjoy. This is most likely the tunes that are quite easy for you to play and will make you feel good about yourself.

Jump into the fire: Open your book to the latest page that is be-deviling you. If it seems too daunting, listen to the audio. Then, look at the first measure or two. Can you "drag" yourself through that much of it? If so, you've taken a huge step forward! Stick with this small section before moving on to any more of this difficult piece. Play it over and over *at least 8 times*, maybe more. There is probably some particular area of two to three notes where you are tripping up again and again. Zero in on that area and see if there is a finger out of place or an unusual finger placement. Once you tackle this little section, you may find that it reoccurs in other parts of the tune, so you may have solved more than one problem area without even knowing it. If you can get further into this challenging new section of the book by going "a measure at a time", then so much the better. This activity might take a good twenty minutes, which will leave you about half an hour to go.

Work on memorization: Pick a tune you can play really well. Perhaps you are still reading the tablature, but you can play it like a champ when you are reading it. Try closing the book and see if you can play it without your "crutch." You may get through the first couple of measures and then it may start to break down and get a little "hazy." One method that works well for me when I *have* to memorize something, is to make a recording of myself.

First, play through the song while reading it. Then, record yourself playing the tune *while* reading it from the book. Remember before you play it to give yourself a count-off so you are ready to play along with the recording you are about to make. Assuming you played it correctly on the recording, the next step is to close the book, turn on the recording, and try playing along. This helps you "psychologically" to push your memory further, because you know you *can* play it. It is just a matter of *picturing* yourself playing it correctly. It works for me every time. This little exercise could easily take up fifteen to twenty minutes.

Last ten minutes: If you feel too burned out from what you've had to do for the last fifty or so minutes, go ahead and play your "best stuff" and enjoy yourself for the last ten minutes. This would be a good time to try playing along with the guitar accompaniment on the audio download. You could also record yourself playing your best stuff. When listening to your recordings ask the following: Is your timing consistent? Are your notes and chords coming out clear? Do you "slow down" in the tougher spots? Be critical but don't be too hard on yourself. After all, for many of you beginners, you are making decent-sounding music for the first time. Tomorrow is another day, and you *will* make progress. Save those recordings you made today, then in a month, compare them to what you sounded like today. I think you'll be amazed at the difference you hear!

EXERCISES TO STRETCH YOUR ABILITIES

The Eight Times ("8X") Pages—Part Two

Play each repeat section "8X" then move on. Intensive practice like this is what is called "woodshedding."

Now would be a good time to review the "8X Pages—Part One!" (Page 44)

A Summary of Licks from the Book

Next is one massive exercise featuring "cherry-picked" licks you have come across in this book. Here are a few things to watch out for:

- The barres at both 7th and 5th frets

- Rhythm: When and when not to pause

- What lick is for what chord

- Varied amounts of repeated measures: Mostly two, sometimes just one, and sometimes four.

For G (both measures)

For G (both measures)

5 For D or D7
Barre 7th fret

For G
ind

For C
Barre 5th fret

For G

9 For D
Barre 7th fret

For G
ind

For G (both measures)

13 For C (both measures)
(C chord down)

(Single notes – for C)

For G (both measures)

17 For D or D7 (both measures)

(D7 chord down)

For G (both measures)

(4th!)

21 For C (both measures)

(C chord down)

For G (both measures)

25 For G (1 measure)

For C (1 measure)

For C (1 measure)
mid   mid

For G (1 measure)

(Continues)

29   D7 (D7 chord down)   To: G   D7 (D7 chord down)   To: G

33   For D or D7   G   For D or D7   To: G

37   For G   To: C (C chord down)   To: D7 (D7 chord down)   To: G

41   For G   To: C (C chord down)   To: D7 (D7 chord down) To: G

45   For G   To: C (C chord down)   To: D7   To: G

49   For G   To: C   To: D7   To: G
                      Barre 5th fret   Barre 7th fret   ind

You are now ready *(I hope)* for your final exam.

It will start with a "16-Measure Chord Progression," showing you a basic accompaniment through it. After that, it will continue in the form of mixing and matching the licks you have been practicing. They are placed in a logical order that the chords for the progression call for. *(Keep in mind, that this particular assemblage of licks was an arbitrary choice of mine.)* There are practically infinite combinations of how these various licks can be assembled.

Final Exam

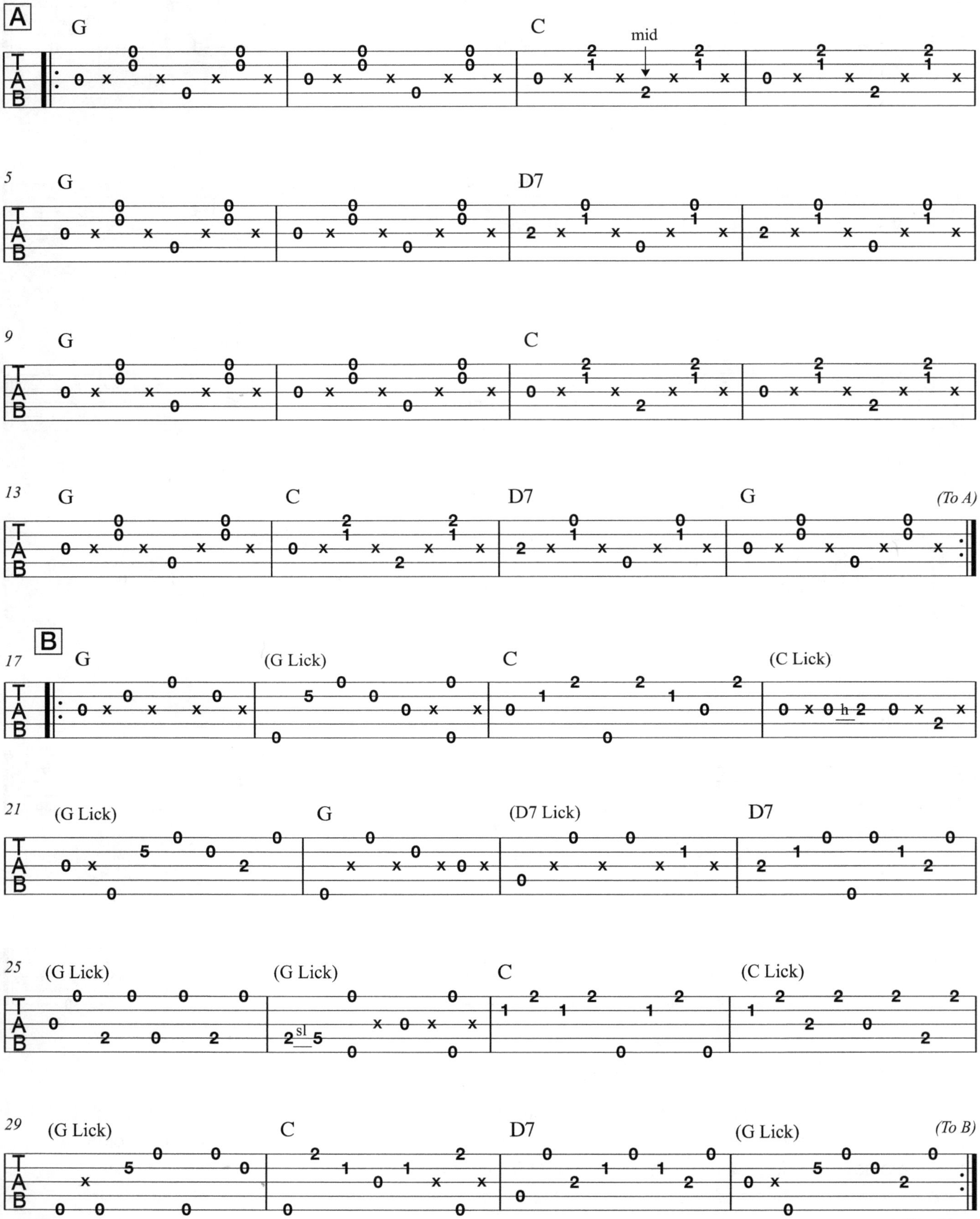

(Continues)

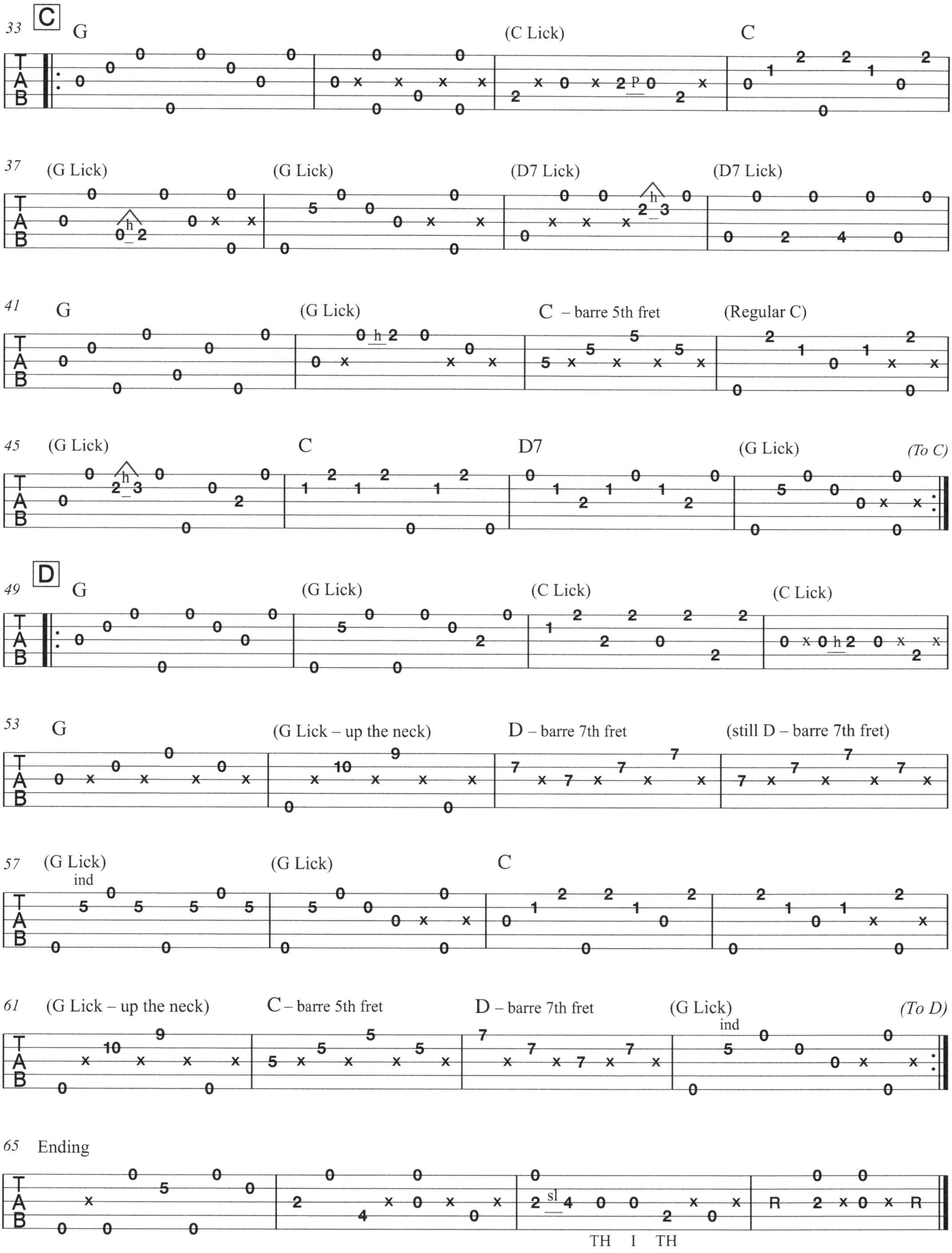
C
G
(C Lick)
C
(G Lick)
(G Lick)
(D7 Lick)
(D7 Lick)
G
(G Lick)
C – barre 5th fret
(Regular C)
(G Lick)
C
D7
(G Lick)
(To C)
D
G
(G Lick)
(C Lick)
(C Lick)
G
(G Lick – up the neck)
D – barre 7th fret
(still D – barre 7th fret)
(G Lick)
ind
(G Lick)
C
(G Lick – up the neck)
C – barre 5th fret
D – barre 7th fret
(G Lick)
ind
(To D)
Ending
TH I TH

CHAPTER 14

SUPPLEMENTAL TUNES

The next five tunes are a preview of the kind of material you will find in Volume 2 of this series. "Cripple Creek" is, of course, a banjo classic that is arranged in as many different ways as there are banjo players on the planet. So, no doubt, you will see another version of "Cripple Creek" in the next book.

"Look Ma, No Left Hand" is an original tune of mine in which the initial melodies (Parts A and B) are both played with just the picking hand. When I wrote the variations (A1 and B1), I couldn't resist bringing in a couple of "fretted" notes—but I do give you fair warning when they occur. Enjoy these last five and I hope to be with you again in Volume 2.

CRIPPLE CREEK (Version 1)

Arranged by Jeff Belding

(Notice the "delay" to the slides caused by the pause.)

After completing the chord part, return to the top of the page and play the melody again.

LOOK MA, NO LEFT HAND*

By Jeff Belding

Banjo tune on Open Strings (pretty much …)

* I apologize to my left-handed banjo picker friends—I know it's "Look Ma, No Right Hand" for you.

WAY BACK WHEN

By Jeff Belding

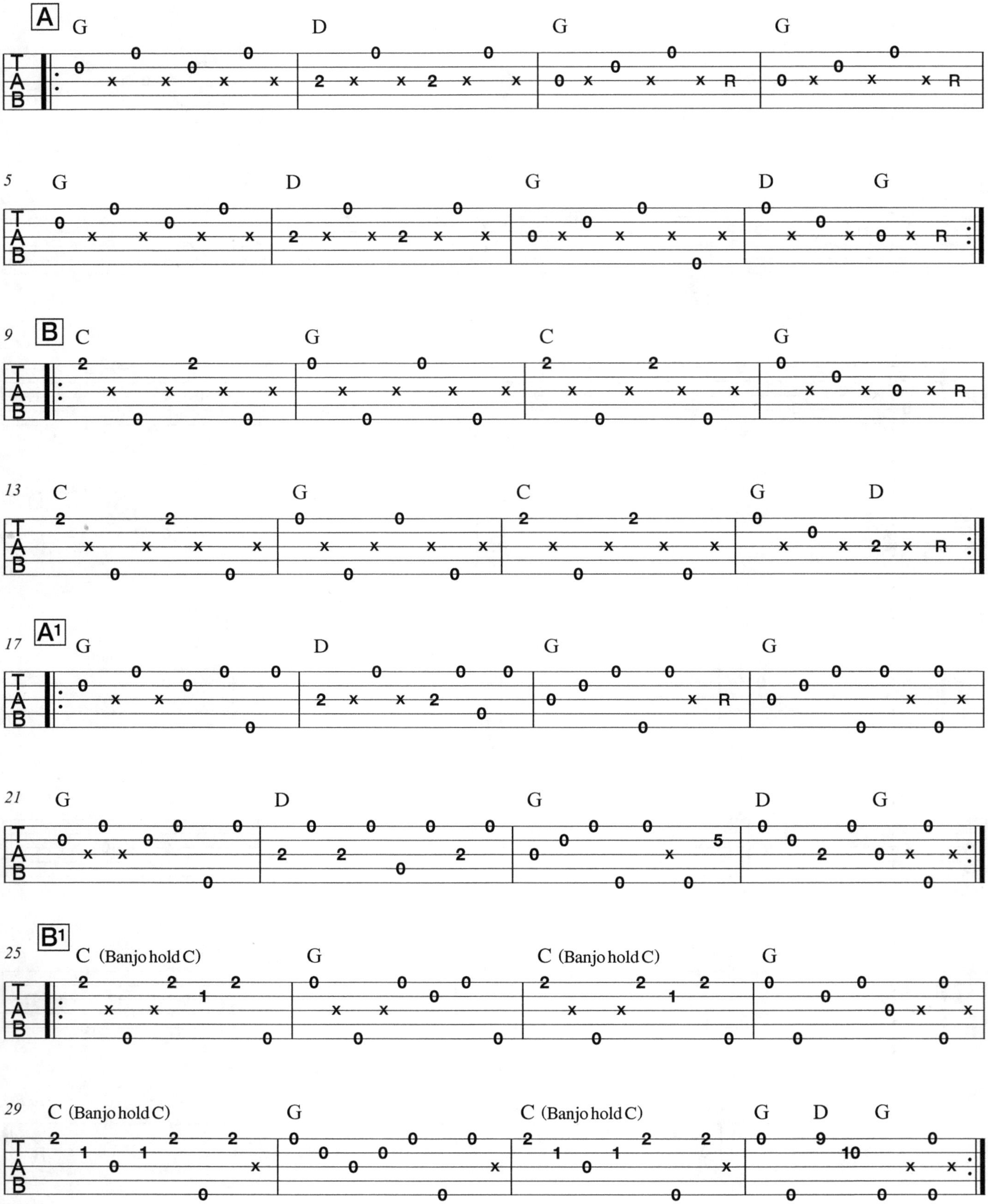

D CHORD RAMBLE

By Jeff Belding

You thought you were done with D chords? They're baaack!

IMPRESS YOUR PICKER FRIENDS

By Jeff Belding

APPENDIX A
Accompaniments for Tunes in the Book

Chord charts for the songs listed below are available for download from my website *musicalongtheway.com*. You will hear these on the audio as played by the guitar and, in some cases, the banjo. The charts are written in standard notation for "rhythm guitar."

Each slash line (/) represents one beat of a measure where either a single note is picked, or multiple strings are strummed (for banjo, two-string plucks). In the first measure of the very first song ("Fretting Fingers Workout") you are shown what the guitar and the banjo are doing to play these accompaniments. The songs are arranged in two sections. Section One contains songs with four beats per measure and Section Two, songs with three beats per measure. It's highly recommended that you try to play *all* of these accompaniments on your banjo. It is a skill you will need when you sit in to jam with others.

Section 1 • Tunes with Four Beats per Measure

Fretting Fingers Workout

"Ode to Joy"

"Long, Long Ago"

"Can Can"; "Simple Gifts"

"Camptown Races"; Higher Notes

Banjo Exercise I

How to Use Banjo Imitato

"Oh! Susanna"

Banjo Exercise II

"Shortnin' Bread"

Banjo Rocking Exercise

"Red River Valley"

"Look Ma, No Left Hand"

Final Exam

"Cripple Creek"

Section 2 • Tunes with Three Beats per Measure

"The Irish Washerwoman"

"Garry Owen"

"Home on the Range"

APPENDIX B
More About Tuning

Fine tuning an instrument has a lot to do with comparing the sound of two notes on different strings. Assuming the fourth string (the thickest string) has been tuned to the correct pitch, the following should be true:

Both G   Both B   Both D   Both High G

Should match in pitch   Should match in pitch   Should match in pitch   Should match in pitch

The previous is the typical tuning system used for most fretted stringed instruments, especially before electronic tuners existed.

The following is an "open string" system that many find to be more accurate than the system shown above. Below are the opening notes for three tunes that you are probably familiar with.

These song snippets give you the sense of pitch relationships of pairs or groups of strings "ringing together" in good harmony. As you become more familiar with these tunes, your subconscious will absorb these sounds, and one day, you *will* become better at tuning your banjo. I like to start my tuning process on the *low* D or 4th (thickest) string. I pair that up with the G or 3rd string and I get:

1   Here Comes the Bride

(Slow ------------)   (Quicker)

Here   comes   the   bride...   (Listen for the 4th to 3rd string relationship.)

2   Red River Valley

From   this   va l   -   ley   they   say...   (etc.)

(Listen for the relationship of the first 3 notes ringing together.)

3   Star Spangled Banner

(Listen for the ring of the 1st and 5th strings.)

Oh, _____   say   can   you   see...   (etc.)

APPENDIX C
What Is a Lick?

It is a series of the same notes that may appear several times at various parts of a song or instrumental tune.

The follow-up question would often be:

"How does a *lick* differ from a *run* or *fill* or *phrase* or *walk-up* or *roll?*"

A *lick*, *fill*, *run*, or *phrase* and *walk-up* are pretty much interchangeable terms. Which one do you like the sound of? Then go ahead and use *that* one. I sometimes use the different terms to help me remember how to categorize certain groups of recurring notes in my head.

Then – "What is a roll"?

A *roll* is a repeating series of strings, picked by a repeating finger pattern in the picking hand. There is very little (and often times *nothing*) going on with the fretting hand, when playing a banjo "roll."

Jeff performing with the band "Out of the Bluegrass" — Mac Petrequin on banjo,
Bert Wilson on bass, and Pete Conklin on mandolin — all have been students of Jeff's.

About the Author

Jeff Belding studied at the Boston Conservatory, the New England Conservatory and the College of Saint Rose, where he received a Bachelor of Science Degree in Studio Music. He has also studied banjo extensively with Bill Keith and Roger Sprung.

He is an award-winning multi-instrumentalist and plays banjo, guitar, mandolin, bass, fiddle, piano, and drums. His career has given him a diverse background in bluegrass, country, jazz and classical music styles. He has performed with many bands, as well as in musicals and has an equally wide range of studio recording projects, including performing on and producing albums and movie soundtracks.

Jeff won first place in the New Twists for Banjo contest judged by Tony Trischka and was nominated Instrumentalist-of-the-Year by the Northeast Country Music Association.

His most recent work in live music includes: Out of the Bluegrass (traditional-sounding bluegrass with a modern twist), Saratoga Faire (Celtic music, with a "renaissance" flair) and the Craig Thaler Group (acoustic instrumental bluegrass and jazz). His professional work in these groups has found him in concert halls, weddings, renaissance festivals, fairgrounds, and (not to mention) gin mills.

Jeff has been a music instructor in the Hudson Valley and New York's Capital District for over 40 years.

One of his favorite pastimes is camping and jamming at bluegrass festivals with friends and strangers alike.

www.ingramcontent.com/pod-product-compliance
Lightning Source LLC
Chambersburg PA
CBHW062053090426
42740CB00016B/3123